Exodus

WEIDENFELD & NICOLSON

BOB MARLEY & THE WAILERS

EXILE 1977

EDITED BY RICHARD WILLIAMS

A wall painting in Ocho Rios on
Jamaica's north coast, not far from
Bob Marley's birthplace in the
parish of St Ann.

Thirty years after its first appearance, and almost a decade after it was nominated by *Time* magazine as the Album of the Century, *Exodus* continues to convey the clearest possible impression of Bob Marley – the singer, the lyricist, the musician, the bandleader, the philosopher, the lover, the icon of a people – at the height of his remarkable powers.

By the time he came to make it, the initial battle for the recognition of reggae had been won. Thanks in large part to Marley's efforts, the music of a small Caribbean island had become an international language; in the process, he had earned worldwide acclamation as its foremost exponent. But the battle for survival was just beginning. Having narrowly escaped a hail of bullets in Jamaica, he arrived in London in the first week of 1977 and set to work on his fifth studio album.

This book describes how and why, at the age of 32 and in the fullness of his creative maturity, he chose the theme of redemption in its many forms: the spiritual redemption of his fellow descendants of the African diaspora and of mankind in general in the awesomely powerful title track in 'One Love', the redemptive power of sexual attraction in 'Turn Your Lights Down Low' and of romantic ardour in 'Waiting in Vain'.

Lloyd Bradley outlines a story that began with an assassination attempt and ended with a peace concert, events that sandwiched the extraordinarily fruitful encounter between Marley and an emerging movement of disaffected British youth: the 'punky reggae party', as he called it, which took place in London in the year of the Queen's Silver Jubilee. Vivien Goldman describes the mood of excitement surrounding the recording sessions in two West London basement studios.

Richard Williams reconstructs an impromptu football match that interrupted the sessions and illustrates Marley's love of the game. Robert Christgau looks at how *Exodus* helped Marley to increase his audience in the United States and to win over the sceptics, including the author. Neil Spencer remembers the atmosphere at the historic concert during which Marley persuaded Jamaica's warring politicians to link hands, if only for a moment. And Linton Kwesi Johnson examines the poetry of Marley's lyrics, with their biblical allusions and rich borrowings from the street.

Defiant in the face of adversity, suffused with yearning for a state of heavenly grace on earth, *Exodus* stands as the definitive statement of the concerns and the artistry of a man who, while himself marked by many of humanity's imperfections, rose from the obscurity of a Third World shanty town to become one of the 20th century's most beloved and inspiring figures, with a message that speaks across the generations to people of every colour and creed. This is how it came to pass.

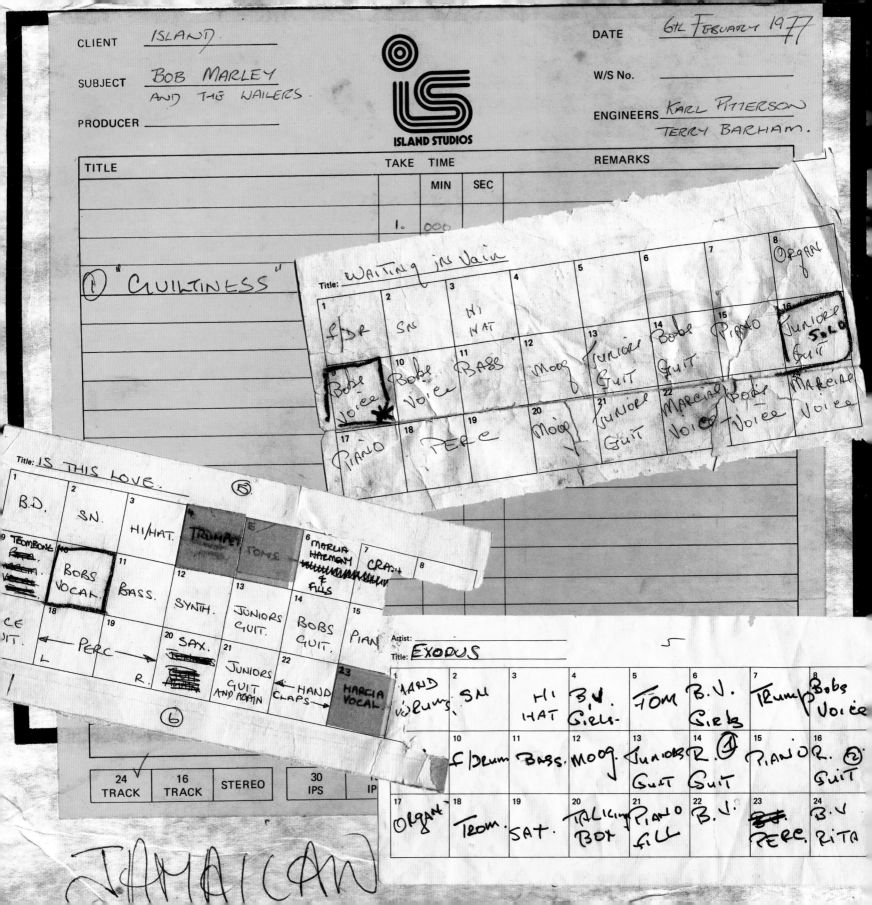

A SENSE OF MOMENTUM

CHRIS BLACKWELL

When an artist is really hot, they're surrounded by a special kind of energy. And that kind of energy was all around Bob Marley when he arrived in London with the tracks that would become *Exodus*. **It was his time.**

Bob and I had begun our collaboration in 1972, with *Catch a Fire*. Five years later, everything he had worked towards seemed to come together in the period surrounding *Exodus*, even though it began, in December 1976, when he was wounded by shots from an intruder at his home in Kingston, Jamaica. The incident took place on the eve of the Smile Jamaica concert, in which his appearance was intended to help heal the divisions between the island's two main political factions. Within days of the concert he had left Jamaica and arrived in the UK, and his escape seemed to create a kind of hyper-energy that was amplified by the vibrant scene he found in London. I think this was the first time he had felt really important – not in a conceited way, but in the knowledge that he was on the right track. Combined with the development of his songwriting and the evolution of his band, it gave a very powerful sense of momentum to his work.

The way our arrangement worked was that he would record the tracks and I would mix them and select a running order for the album. The songs that became *Exodus* and its successor, *Kaya*, were recorded at the same time. Bob handed them over to me, and I was the person who separated them into two albums. We didn't talk about the mixing or the sequencing a great deal. Our relationship wasn't based on hanging out or chatting a lot. We communicated, I suppose, through the music. Instead of describing in words what I was thinking, I'd put it together and play it for him.

Exodus was Bob's fifth studio album for Island, and by that time he was filling every bit of space on the multi-track tape – horns going this way, voices going that way. Part of my job was to pare things away so that you could hear what was at the core of it. I always felt that if you could hear the rhythm in the front all the time, and then the colouring of the horns here and the voices there, it would just seduce you.

Many of the tracks completely blew me away – 'The Heathen', because it was a very different type of thing, not at all traditional reggae; the bass-line feel of 'Natural Mystic'; the fantastic

THINGS WERE REALLY HAPPENING FOR HIM. HE WAS MAKING IT, HE WAS FEELING GREAT, AND THAT ENERGY CAME ACROSS IN THE BOUNCE AND THE FEEL OF THE TRACKS.

energy of the song 'Exodus'; the beautiful melody of 'Waiting in Vain'. He was allowing new influences to reshape the music. I think he was very confident at that time, and the more confident you are, the more you can let your influences come forward.

If you think of the songs as a complete piece of work, they contain fewer political songs and a greater proportion of love songs and happy songs than any of his records before – and for a reason, in my opinion. Things were good. Things

On a trip to Rio de Janeiro to celebrate the opening of Island Records' Brazilian office in March 1980, a quartet including Bob Marley and Chris Blackwell pose for the camera of the actress Nathalie Delon: from left, the Wailers' guitarist Junior Marvin, Marley, Inner Circle singer Jacob Miller, and Blackwell. During the visit Marley met the footballer Paulo Cesar, a member of Brazil's 1970 World Cup winning team, and joined in a match played on a pitch owned by the celebrated singer, novelist and occasional football reporter Chico Buarque. Two days later, having returned home to Jamaica, Jacob Miller would die in a car crash on Hope Road, not far from Marley's house.

were really happening for him. He was making it, he was feeling great, and that energy came across in the bounce and the feel of the tracks. I felt, however, that there were several killer songs that had more political or sociological relevance to them, so I decided to lead the first album with them. The intention was to open up by banging you on the head with songs like 'Guiltiness' and 'So Much Things to Say' and then – after 'Exodus' itself, which is the heart of the album – you'd turn over to side two (in the original vinyl LP format, that is) and start dancing and mellowing out with 'Jamming', 'Waiting in Vain', 'Turn Your Lights Down Low', 'Three Little Birds' and 'One Love'.

I thought *Exodus* was the album that would definitely break it wide open for him. He was like the most anticipated rock star of the time. This was 1977, remember: mainstream rock had become a little bit stale, and punk was just starting. Bob was something very, very different. And when *Exodus* appeared, it was like Jimi Hendrix coming out with *Electric Ladyland*. There was a feeling that people couldn't wait to hear what he'd done.

Time magazine nominated it as the Album of the Century, ahead of Miles Davis' *Kind of Blue* and Hendrix's *Are You Experienced*. Does it stand out for me from the rest of Bob's output? In an overall way, probably it does. But it's close. *Catch a Fire* is fantastic, an experiment in blending different kinds of music that just about came off, thanks to its solid roots. And I think *Survival*, which came a couple of years after *Exodus*, is fantastic, too. But, of them all, probably *Exodus* is the one that is the most dead-centre. I am overjoyed to know that today, 30 years after Bob wrote and recorded it, the album continues to have such a profound effect on listeners old and new.

*Chris Blackwell is the founder of Island Records. Having picked up several of their early 45s for UK release in the 1960s, he signed Bob Marley and the Wailers to the label in 1972 and co-produced all their recordings until Bob's death in 1981.

Music played an increasingly vital role in the daily lives of Jamaicans in the 1970s.

Left: A typical Kingston mobile record shack.

Right: A pressing plant on Maxfield Avenue. Bob Marley's Tuff Gong operation included a record shack which sold 45s released on his own label.

When the Wailers returned to London at the beginning of 1977, the UK's punk/new wave movement was gathering momentum. Many of the more conscious punks responded to reggae, seeing its raw honesty as the antithesis of disco's mirror-ball artifice. In his turn, Bob Marley welcomed their acceptance. Whether he quite got the point of the punks is not entirely clear, since 'Punky Reggae Party', the song he wrote and recorded in celebration of the new alliance, contains exhortations to 'groove!' and 'please don't be naughty!', neither of which would get much recognition from the denizens of the Roxy. But the song finds him naming the bands with whom he makes common cause – 'The Jam, the Damned, the Clash, Maytals will be there, Dr Feelgood too' – and giving voice to the sort of sentiments they undoubtedly had in common: 'Rejected by society, treated with impunity, protected by my dignity, I search for reality.' The Wailers' musicianship set them apart from the majority of the punk bands, and it was the power of their live shows that spread their reputation beyond the original hard core of their admirers.

THE STORY OF EXODUS

LLOYD BRADLEY

The *Exodus* album could only have happened in London in 1977. While it may be filed under 'reggae' in music stores, as an album it owes more to Kensington than it does to Kingston and is so much a product of the year it was made that the *Time* magazine accolade of album of the century becomes even more remarkable. It was all a matter of luck, too. That's 'luck' as defined in an old West African saying that states: 'Luck is what happens when preparation meets opportunity.'

Bob Marley had been preparing to make an album like *Exodus* for the better part of 20 years, since he first stood in front of a microphone as a teenager at the start of the 1960s, when he was clearly thinking beyond the parochiality of sound system hits and the early-period Wailers' Impressions impression, riddled with cover versions. In the 10 years that followed, he was exposed to all manner of music by his American manager, was disciplined by the straitjacketed Kingston studio system, lived in several different countries and worked extensively with Jamaica's most free-thinking producer. Then he signed to a progressive, international, but still independent record label that understood perfectly how the

words 'reggae musician' and 'rock star potential' didn't have to be mutually exclusive. As all these past events collided with the developments taking place in every other aspect of Marley's life, *Exodus* couldn't have been prepared for better.

As regards the opportunity, that's where London at that particular time became vital to this equation. The British capital in 1977 was unique in the way its music and youth culture

of circumstances that brought about Bob Marley's exile to London, which could not have been more at odds with the positivity and all-round upfullness of the record. So it's both a massive irony and supreme statement of Marley's character that without the horrifying incident in which he and his family and friends were attacked and shot in his own home, the album might never have existed. Or at least not as we know it.

WITHOUT THE HORRIFYING INCIDENT IN WHICH HE AND HIS FAMILY AND FRIENDS WERE ATTACKED AND SHOT IN HIS OWN HOME, THE ALBUM MIGHT NEVER HAVE EXISTED

---

were developing, encouraging a group such as the Wailers to push the boundaries of their own endeavours. Alongside all this creative freedom, London offered an all-important personal space in a way their homeland never could.

Perhaps the most astonishing thing about the creation of *Exodus*, however, is the arrangement

On the steps of the front door of the house at 56 Hope Road was where Marley could be found day after day, reasoning with old and new friends. In an uptown location a stone's throw from the Prime Minister's residence, it was a place in which he never failed to keep faith with his downtown roots.

1 TRAPPED IN A WAR ZONE

The Jamaica that Bob Marley left at the end of 1976 on his way to Britain was so far removed from the popular notion of a laid-back island paradise that the swaying palms and carefree couples on the tourist board posters might as well have been a mirage. The brochures' white sandy beaches were indeed deserted; tourism had all but dried up under the darkening shadows of the mayhem consuming the island's capital.

In the run-up to the general elections, scheduled for the end of that year, politically motivated violence in Kingston was responsible for around 200 killings, plus beatings, gang rapes and fire-bombings of homes and businesses. For ordinary Jamaicans there was nothing romantic or even revolutionary about this degree of sufferation as large parts of their city became undeclared war zones. 'Soldiers' representing the country's two political parties terrorized entire communities; they shot it out with each other and with the official army against a backdrop of tanks on the streets during the day and helicopter searchlights raking the lanes and alleyways after dark to make sure the curfew was observed.

Political violence was nothing remotely new in Jamaican life. The island has a long and distinguished tradition of slave uprisings and guerrilla warfare against the plantations, and the first half of the 20th century was peppered with revolt and rebellion as the people regularly took to the streets to confront authority. In the mid-1960s,

As the kind of random criminal violence endemic to any Third World conurbation became organized and orchestrated, it had the effect of redefining ghetto communities as virtual garrisons. Horrific as this situation might have been, the street skirmishes of that decade did little to prepare the city's population for the sheer scale of the brutality that followed

THE CRIMINAL GANGS OPERATING IN THE SLUMS OF WEST KINGSTON WERE RECRUITED BY THE JAMAICAN LABOUR PARTY AND ITS RIVAL PEOPLE'S NATIONAL PARTY, ARMED FROM A FLOOD OF CONTRABAND WEAPONRY AND PUT TO WORK INTIMIDATING EACH OTHER'S POTENTIAL VOTERS

however, matters took an altogether chilling turn. The criminal gangs operating in the slums of West Kingston were recruited by the Jamaican Labour Party and its rival People's National Party, armed from a flood of contraband weaponry and put to work intimidating each other's potential voters.

in the 1970s. By then, in the wake of a government programme of progressive socialism that had gone badly wrong, senior politicians were increasingly entrenched in polemic and embroiled in Jamaica's economic collapse, thus any social and political aspirations had fallen apart before they got going.

The most infamous symbol of the Jamaican government's 'heavy-manners regime' was the Gun Court, into which those found in possession of firearms were thrown. Marley passed through those red-painted gates, visiting an incarcerated friend.

With hindsight it's easy to look beyond the optimism of Jamaica's Independence celebrations in 1962 and see that so much of value on the island had been sold off by the British before they left – chiefly the bauxite, tourism and banana industries. Indeed, the former colonial power wasn't giving Jamaicans anything much, or anything other than the potential for a crippling balance of trade, an unsustainable infrastructure and a population increasingly less able to support itself. Food and petrol shortages were commonplace; unemployment ran at nearly 40 per cent; declining trade and tourism reduced the influx of foreign currency; Prime Minister Michael Manley's cosying up to Cuba's Fidel Castro meant US aid dollars were withheld; and those of the skilled and educated classes who weren't heading for Miami themselves made sure that any money they had was. A dozen or so years on, the lowering of the Union flag was not so much a new beginning as the beginning of the end.

Under such circumstances it's almost understandable that a generation of ghetto youth, who knew Independence as nothing other than a source of frustration and disappointment, should see gunslinging as a feasible option. As a career choice it offered pretty much everything the new government had promised its young people back in 1962 when the British packed up and left: a sense of belonging... cash... access to imported modern technology (the AK47 and the M16)... encouragement of self-help with a blind eye being turned to whatever gainful crime was committed under the mayhem... the respect of your peers... opportunity for promotion... all that was lacking was a pension plan, but then you probably wouldn't live long enough to collect on it anyway. Fired up by the fierce partisan rhetoric from each party leader, as the lack of comprehensible solutions to this mess meant policy statement was replaced by open aggression, it was hardly a quantum leap from disillusion to anarchy.

In 1974 the killing was so far out of control that the government passed the Suppression of Crime Act, outlawing firearms and calling for them to be handed in at police stations. Like so many of Manley's well-meaning policies, this backfired spectacularly. As might have been expected, it was only the law-abiding citizens who gave up their guns. Not only did they feel more vulnerable immediately after this firearms amnesty, the sharp rise in the number of murders and recorded shootings in the city in the following weeks fully justified their fears. The Gun Court Act followed later that year, and was Prince Buster's Judge Dread come to life. The act provided for unwarranted searches of property and person, incarceration without bail and mandatory 'indefinite detention' for those caught in possession of a gun, a bullet or even a spent cartridge. All of this took place in a purpose-built, self-contained court and jailhouse complex encompassed by barbed wire and known as the Gun Court.

The most remarkable thing about this institution was that it was painted blood red. In the name of something he called 'behavioural change', Michael Manley had employed a team of psychia-

trists and sociologists to pick the colour scheme most likely to convince inmates and outsiders alike that crime doesn't pay. Fairly quickly, the compound became nicknamed 'Stalag 17', after the William Holden POW movie of that name, but the other frequent comparison was with the town of Lago, the scene of Clint Eastwood's existential western *High Plains Drifter*. A huge hit in Jamaican cinemas the previous year, the film's central character was a ruthless and nameless gunman who forced the population to paint every building in the town a very similar shade of red, although his reason was less complicated than the Prime Minister's: 'So it looks like Hell.'

Whatever it looked like, the simple truth was the Gun Court didn't work. It failed to stem the rising tide of violent unrest wreaked on Kingstonians by people who looked like themselves. From 1974 to 1976 the murder rate almost doubled from 11.5 per 100,000 people to 19.7 (at the time of writing, London's figure was 2.4 and New York's 6.9). In June 1976, Michael Manley's government put the country 'under heavy manners' and declared a state of emergency. The new draconian powers were enforced with such gusto that between their introduction and the general election on December 16 more than 500 people, including some prominent politicians, were detained without trial on the broad-brush charge of 'politically motivated disorder'. Yet still 200 Jamaican citizens managed to lose their lives.

'Wherever there is joy, there is pleasure': devastated by hurricanes and gangsterism, yet possessing some of the world's most beautiful scenery and nurturing a musical idiom that would be heard throughout the world, post-colonial Jamaica was a place of contrasting experiences and aspirations.

Michael Manley, Jamaica's Prime Minister from 1972–80 and 1989–92, attempted to strengthen the nation's ties with Fidel Castro's Cuba, but succeeded only in earning the wrath of the US government and the International Monetary Fund. Guns flooded into the island, arming both sides of the political divide and forcing Manley to impose draconian measures as Kingston descended into a nightmare of bloodshed.

Opposite: A helmeted policeman, his firearm holstered at his side, guards a Kingston bank.

Trenchtown under 'heavy manners' in the mid-1970s.

Top: A roadblock separates the territories of Michael Manley's People's National Party and Edward Seaga's Jamaican Labour Party.

Bottom: Police were occupied in a vain attempt to keep the two sides apart.

Opposite: Available from record shacks such as this one, reggae served a precious function as a commentary on and a relief from the Jamaican situation.

No public event was without its air of latent violence. Here two policeman, one swinging his wooden truncheon, keep an eye on a function at the National Stadium, where the Peace Concert would take place in 1978.

EVEN IF MARLEY HAD BEEN THE SORT OF MAN TO USE HIGH WALLS AND GUN-TOTING UNIFORMED GUARDS TO CUT HIMSELF OFF FROM THE PEOPLE, HE STILL WOULDN'T HAVE BEEN IMMUNE TO THE CHAOS PERMEATING PRACTICALLY EVERY ASPECT OF KINGSTON LIFE

2 BULLETS FLY UPTOWN

Any idea that this unrest was going on downtown and therefore wouldn't touch an international superstar like Bob Marley is, of course, nonsense. Even if Marley had been the sort of man to use high walls and gun-toting uniformed guards to cut himself off from the people, he still wouldn't have been immune to the chaos permeating practically every aspect of Kingston life. Nobody was. At one point during that period, many of the city's traffic lights were switched off so cars wouldn't have to stop and thereby put drivers at risk from gunfire. As it was, given that the city's tonier residents were living in a state of apparent siege, Marley seemed to make little effort to take even the most basic Kingston home-security precautions.

He had moved uptown to 56 Hope Road a couple of years previously. His neighbours now included government ministers and foreign diplomats, but the white-walled compound with its colonial-style great house, coach house and sundry outbuildings quickly took on a character unique to the area. What were once grounds became a bona fide yard, populated by Marley's dread associates and alive with music, reasoning sessions and an almost continuous game of football. Old friends and new acquaintances came up from downtown to hang out, to gawp or to hold their hands out – Marley's generosity was well known. It would've been impossible to keep track of all the people coming and going during the course of an average day, even if there ever was such a thing as an 'average' day at 56 Hope Road.

In spite of the obvious personal safety issues, this was exactly how Bob Marley wanted it, and it speaks volumes about him. On one level he had always been a Man of the People; yet pragmatically, he was well aware that as a Jamaican popular entertainer he couldn't afford to be anything else. As a righteous Rastaman he was determined he should live life as it is supposed to be lived – with trust and openness – and not how other less salubrious elements would force people to exist. It was his belief that people would respond to how they were treated; thus everybody from ghetto sufferers to political warlords and members of the Jamaican cabinet had a place in his yard. At the same time, Marley's ego assumed he was above danger, that the people – his people – would do him no harm. For a long time this trusting attitude was rewarded. Although

The house at 56 Hope Road was a colonial residence that became the home of Jamaica's most famous son. After Chris Blackwell gave it to Marley as part of the *Catch a Fire* deal, it became the place where all the Wailers' business was conducted, including that of the Tuff Gong record company, whose delivery van can be seen in the left foreground. And it was where, on the evening of December 3, 1976, during rehearsals for the Smile Jamaica concert, three gunmen broke in and sprayed the bullets that wounded Marley, his manager Don Taylor, and his wife, Rita.

never less than aware of the perpetual tension outside the walls, the Marley camp – and there's no other way to describe it – was an oasis of peace, harmony and the celebration of life. Sure, there was a discreet security presence – nobody was naive enough to feel completely untouchable – but largely they were left alone. Unfortunately, such a situation was not to last.

While it did, however, a primary reason for this status quo rested on Marley's careful non-alignment in the deadly arena of Jamaican party politics. In the run up to the 1972 election he had openly backed Michael Manley's pro-Rasta platform by appearing as part of the PNP's Musical Bandwagon (a concert tour of reggae artists, including Dennis Brown, Clancy Eccles and Max Romeo, banging, quite literally, the party drum). This time around, with the city a primed powder keg and the singer himself on the verge of international superstardom, the stakes were far too high. Plus although Manley won in 1972 with the help of a surprisingly large Rasta vote, he had conspicu-

ALTHOUGH NEVER LESS THAN AWARE OF THE PERPETUAL TENSION OUTSIDE THE WALLS, THE MARLEY CAMP – AND THERE'S NO OTHER WAY TO DESCRIBE IT – WAS AN OASIS OF PEACE, HARMONY AND THE CELEBRATION OF LIFE

ously, if perhaps understandably, failed to deliver on his two key promises to them – legalising ganja and providing assisted repatriation to Ethiopia. Thus the island's dreads felt let down and were opting to leave the 'politricks' to Babylon at this election.

Given his international status, Bob Marley's perceived endorsement of either party would be of huge value and by the end of 1976 the PNP had managed to drag him on to their side. Or at least they seemed to have, when Michael Manley co-opted a grand and heartfelt gesture the singer was planning for the island's people.

For months Marley had been talking about doing something to raise Jamaicans' spirits, and proposed to play a free concert that would be readily accessible to the ghetto crowds. Called, in typically optimistic Bob Marley fashion, Smile Jamaica, at the very least it would provide a night's respite from the madness that had taken over daily life downtown. Merely to be seen to be participating in such a show would be a powerful campaign boost as the election loomed, and

immediately it was announced that both parties had approached him to get involved. Regardless of the unsullied nature of Marley's intentions, for an event of this scale government cooperation would be required, therefore excluding the ruling PNP was never going to be an option. The cynicism with which Prime Minister Michael Manley manipulated the event, however, was breathtaking.

After his offer to provide the grounds of Jamaica House, the former prime ministerial mansion, was rejected because it would redefine the show as a government gig, and because the location was too uptown, Manley, who had been delaying the announcement of the election date, then pulled his master stroke. Immediately after the concert date was announced as December 5, the government scheduled December 16 as polling day. The show was already being publicised as a co-production between Marley and Jamaica's cultural office; now it was being repositioned as an ostensible part of Manley's appease-the-people manifesto. Outwardly stoic, Marley was secure in the purity

of his motives and voiced no objections beyond his inner circle. Others, however, weren't so accepting. Following mysterious phone calls 'advising' him to pull out of the show, on the evening of December 3, two white Datsun saloons roared into the Hope Road compound, decanting a trio of gunmen spraying bullets with deadly intent. When the smoke cleared, Bob's wife Rita Marley had a bullet nestling between her scalp and skull; his manager Don Taylor had a bullet in his thigh and one dangerously close to his spine; Lewis Simpson, a friend of the band, had been shot in the stomach; and Marley himself was down after a bullet grazed his chest and lodged in his left arm. Among those who escaped injury were Antonio 'Gilly' Gilbert, the Wailers' cook, and two members of the Wailers' rhythm section, bass guitarist Aston 'Family Man' Barrett and his brother Carlton, the group's drummer, who fled as bullets were fired into the adjacent rehearsal room.

Even a city with as energetic a gun crime situation as Kingston 1976 was stunned. No one has ever been held officially responsible, although

rumours of ghetto justice were rife. Nobody has even come up with a definitive reason as to why it happened – politics, racetrack scams and general gangsterism are the most-mentioned options. But the shooting had one almost unimaginable consequence: it forced Bob Marley to leave Jamaica, the land he loved deeply, and set up home elsewhere.

After receiving treatment at the scene, Marley was driven up into the hills above Jamaica, to a great house in a spectacular location known as Strawberry Hill. Owned by Chris Blackwell, it would eventually become a hotel. Now it served as a sanctuary for the wounded singer. Wrapped in bandages, and in considerable pain, he still played the Smile Jamaica show. Otherwise the gunmen could have claimed victory and the Marley party would have taken those bullets for nothing. But the affront Marley suffered cut several layers deeper than mere ego or even his commitment to the people: Jamaica had turned on him, on more than one level. The government had taken him to be just one more puppet to be manipulated at will – a

preening Michael Manley was highly visible at the show, brandishing the so-called Rod of Correction, a staff given to him by Emperor Haile Selassie. And downtown had come uptown, not to pay homage or play football or to reason or even to beg a few dollars, but to try and kill Bob Marley.

Whatever way you added it up, it was time to go. Straight after the show Marley and his group took a private plane to Nassau in the Bahamas, where they spent Christmas in a mood of contemplation. In the first week of the new year they left for London.

Above: Kingston street scenes during the years of crisis, when ordinary people lived their lives to a soundtrack of gunfire, as the government and the opposition struggled for supremacy in a political struggle that more closely resembled a gang war.

Opposite: Marley at 56 Hope Road, a ping-pong table nearby but his thoughts seemingly focused on the far distance.

Left: As part of the build-up to the Smile Jamaica concert, Marley wrote a song by that title and recorded it with the Wailers. Released in Jamaica on his own Tuff Gong label, it appeared on Island in the UK.

The view of Kingston at dusk from the verandah of Strawberry Hill, the old house up in the Blue Mountains, owned by Chris Blackwell, to which a wounded Marley was taken for safety after the shooting. At night, the headlights of a car leaving 56 Hope Road for Strawberry Hill could be observed almost all the way up the winding road.

THERE WAS ACTUALLY PLENTY OF REGGAE ON OFFER IN THE UK AT THE BEGINNING OF THE 1970S, BUT IT WAS JANGLINGLY CHEERFUL, STRINGSED-UP AND PURE POLYESTER

Against a backdrop of West London council flats and watched by a pair of policemen, a sound system DJ tests his turntables.

3 REFUGE AND RELAXATION

For Marley, the London in which he touched down was an almost entirely different place from the city that he, Peter Tosh and Bunny Wailer had left just six years previously after enduring several extended stays. 'Enduring' is not too strong a description, either: put up in a series of down-market hotels, where they were left to their own devices for weeks at a time, in cramped, unhealthy conditions with a lack of cooking facilities that made a mockery of a Rasta's living and dietary requirements; and where they felt cold for much of the time. And even worse than such personal discomfort, the trips were more or less a total waste of time from a career point of view.

Back then, with social conditions that had been on the slide since Independence, the Jamaica they were commuting from had reached the point at which a less patient post-colonial generation was starting to rebel. On a cultural level this meant roots reggae was dominating the hipper Jamaican sound systems and the first significant wave of songs reflecting Jamaica's situation was actually making it on to vinyl. A series of Lee Perry-produced roots masterpieces such as

'Duppy Conqueror', 'Trenchtown Rock' and 'Small Axe' had virtually engraved the Wailers' name on the Jamaican hit parade. At the same time, their lyrical approach to the creeping injustices of daily life installed them as the people's heroes. In Britain at that time, however, they assumed no such status.

There was actually plenty of reggae on offer in the UK at the beginning of the 1970s, but it was janglingly cheerful, stringsed-up and pure polyester. Although all over the charts, it was regarded in much the same way as a cat that could smoke a pipe – a mildly amusing novelty, but of no lasting value. The Wailers could hardly have been more out of step with this environment. The only existing outlets for an act as generally uncompromising and as musically demanding were the late-night sound system scene and the specialist record shops, where life operated, pretty much deliberately, as an extension of how things were done in Kingston. Yet for reasons never fully explained their management had opted to attempt to launch the trio squarely into the mainstream, on the back of the American singer Johnny Nash, a fellow client whose strictly saccharine take on the one-drop was exemplified by his hit 'I Can See Clearly Now'. By December 1971 the Wailers had

Scenes from the Notting Hill Carnival. In 1977 the Queen's Silver Jubilee shared the spotlight with the Carnival, but the threat of gun crime in London was so low that no one bothered to prevent a sound system acolyte from posing with a dummy Uzi.

no international record deal, no real prospects of live work in the UK and absolutely no money whatsoever. They were only able to buy air tickets out of that cruel British winter because Chris Blackwell, the Jamaican-born proprietor of Island Records, fronted them some cash as part of the advance for the album that would become *Catch A Fire* – a gesture that was itself a breakthrough, since advances for albums, although common practice in the rock world, had not hitherto been a part of deals between record companies and reggae musicians.

But when Marley came back to the UK in 1977, he arrived with the assurance that his standing in the former motherland was almost on a level with the ranking he enjoyed in Jamaica: healthy European sales figures were taken as read; he was starting to trouble the American charts; and this was two years on from the triumphant concert in

London's Lyceum Theatre, after which he had been adopted by the UK media to such a degree that, as far as the mainstream was concerned, Bob Marley *was* reggae. It's a mark of how seriously he and what he did were taken in Britain by then that not only did his shooting make the BBC television news, but it was reported as an 'assassination attempt' rather than a simple attempted murder, with the unmistakeable suggestion of a politically motivated attack.

Although Marley never measured his life in terms of his material wealth, it would be a mistake to assume he wasn't astute enough to recognise the kind of all-round clout that would be ensured by sustained success, and how that would repay him in terms of creative opportunity. Returning to England as an acknowledged celebrity, his life was going to be that much easier. This time around the mundanities in his new world would be magically

taken care of: he would never need to worry where the next ital meal was coming from and the cold could be kept at bay by turning the thermostat up. Denise Mills, formerly Chris Blackwell's trusted assistant, assumed the role of managing their daily requirements. It afforded Bob Marley the luxury of being free to do what he did best – make music. It is another great irony of the Exodus sessions that the level of ease and relaxation offered by Marley's London situation allowed him to channel so effectively the residual rage brought on by the circumstances that had taken him there. Bob Marley was a man who had worn his heart on his sleeve for all his adult life, and any post-shooting songs could easily have been little more than a series of spluttering expressions of anger. Instead he had the time and space to focus his feelings in an intelligent and articulate condemnation of violence and injustice.

HE HAD THE TIME AND SPACE TO FOCUS HIS FEELINGS INTO AN INTELLIGENT AND ARTICULATE CONDEMNATION OF VIOLENCE AND INJUSTICE

Above: During their stay in London in the early months of 1977, Marley and the Wailers made a guest appearance at a Bible-reading class.

Opposite: The Carnival wound its way through the streets of Notting Hill, a pageant of dazzling colour and ground-shaking rhythms.

Above, left: Saturday on Portobello
Road in Notting Hill.

Above, right: Soundsystem under
the Westway overpass.

Opposite, top: On a West London
street, an exile contemplates the
dream of Exodus to a promised land.

Opposite, bottom: None of England's
punk bands espoused the cause of
reggae more enthusiastically than
the Clash, the movement's leading
agitprop-rockers.

Reggae musicians were among those who fell foul of the 'sus' law, an ancient statute designed to apprehend vagrants but used by the police in the London of the 1970s as an excuse for stopping and searching young black males. Aswad's second single, 'Three Babylon', reflected their first-person experience of a detested practice.

Opposite: The West London reggae band Aswad, who turned up at Island Records with a raw, unfinished demo tape one lunchtime in 1975. Before long they were promoting their first album on tour with Eddie and the Hot Rods, playing table football with the Wailers and joining Marley at the session which produced 'Punky Reggae Party'.

Top: The members of Matumbi, with Dennis Bovell on the extreme left, in Brixton.

Bottom, left: The Sex Pistols' Johnny Rotten loved reggae, befriended the young Afro-Caribbean photographer Dennis Morris, and turned his next band, Public Image Ltd, into a platform for the exploration for the influence of dub techniques.

Below: The 100 Club, on London's Oxford Street, was one of the places where the punky reggae party began.

Opposite: When Marley needed a support act for the Exodus tour, he chose not Aswad, his Ladbroke Grove disciples, but Steel Pulse, a band from Handsworth in Birmingham, whose music he felt gave a more original take on the experience of Britain's community of young black people.

WINTER IN BABYLON

VIVIEN GOLDMAN

The Exodus sessions took place in two West London studios: a converted Victorian laundry at the back of Island Records' headquarters in St Peter's Square, Chiswick, and a repurposed church in Basing Street, Notting Hill, parallel to the famous Portobello Road Market. From January to April, from winter to spring, wherever the Wailers worked was rammed with their bred'ren and sistr'en and a motley crew of supporters.

As a member of Island's PR staff, with special responsibility for Bob and the Wailers, I had the privilege of scoring his first slew of cover stories, pushing Rastaman Vibration and the Rainbow show. Oddly, this was not easy; at the time, most of the media hoped these raggedy Rastas would remain in their ghettoes. But when the music hit the right ears, the cover stories came.

Everyone at the company was fighting for the Wailers. At the time Island was a pioneering independent record label, designed on a boutique model. Unlike virtually all record companies today, its offices housed almost all aspects of making and selling records. I remember the buzz when the Wailers would come in at maybe four o'clock in the afternoon. Famous for always being first on the tour bus, Bob Marley often led the way through the loading door in the car park to the very basic rehearsal room. Right down the hall lay the canteen with its black and white linoleum floor, archetypal 1970s rubber plants and the well-used fussball table, behind which was the office of the Fallout Shelter recording studio. When the phones were quiet, I wasn't the only worker to nip downstairs to the canteen, hoping to peek round the heavy rehearsal room door and get a quick hit of the Wailers.

Later, as a journalist, I got to be around the Wailers a lot; maybe Bob trusted me in part because he had first got to know me as his publicist. So it happened that while I was working in Jamaica, Bob invited me to stay at 56 Hope Road, his gracious great house in uptown Kingston. At this busy Rasta commune, in an elite street right next door to the Prime Minister's residence, spiritual ital Dread bred'ren rubbed shoulders with deadly downtown dons and foreign musicians and media. Bob was conducting a social experiment: the Rasta nirvana he described to me as 'bringing the ghetto uptown'.

The day after I left, December 3, 1976, has gone down in infamy. Bob was taking a break from rehearsal, eating grapefruit in the new galley kitchen while Family Man led the Zap Pow horns through their parts for the following day's Smile Jamaica concert. The mellow afternoon abruptly turned into a nightmare as three gunmen stormed in, spraying bullets. But in trying to silence the Tuff Gong, they just turned up his volume.

Like the beleaguered Marcus Garvey and Haile Selassie before them, the Wailers split to London, which Bob described to me as 'a second home'. Night after night those precious sessions were attended by a large rotating cast that usually included the members of the young West London reggae band Aswad and their manager Mikey 'Dread' Campbell, King Sounds, the Sons of Jah, Delroy Washington, Lucky Gordon (the excellent Jamaican chef who had won notoriety as Christine Keeler's lover), and Pepe Judah of the Twelve Tribes, the Rasta organization to which Bob belonged.

The quintessential people's poet, Bob fed off the energy of the small community that would be drawn to spend their nights absorbing and, with their ardent vibes, hoping to help the birth of a masterpiece. Just as many much-loved Marley lines are lifted from the Bible or old Jamaican folk wisdom, so his quick ear tuned in to snatches of conversation or street slang, which he would borrow to leaven some thunderous pronouncement. In his songwriting, Bob liked to be not only eternal, but current, too, and while recording Exodus he clearly felt it takes a village to make an album that captures a community's soul.

The Exodus sessions began in the Fallout Shelter. A heavy fire door would slam shut, eliminating the everyday from the basement studio. The control room and mid-size studio were connected by a short, narrow hall where Bob often chose to sing; he liked the echo. With its soundproofed walls of woollen material and bumpy foam, the control room itself was quite grey. Shadowed by the 24-track mixing desk, a step led down to a comfy couch with a ringside view through a large window, as if into an aquarium, of the musicians recording. It was Bob's favourite spot, maybe because in the glass wall you could see the reflection of whoever came through the control room door, before they could see you – a reassuring feeling for someone who'd just been shot in their own home.

When the tracks were ready for fine-tuning, the band shifted operations to Notting Hill, a couple of miles east of St Peter's Square and very different in atmosphere. Listening to *Exodus* (and *Kaya*, too) grow within the womb of Basing Street's brown-carpeted walls felt like being in mission control; like the whole extended family really were going on a journey, our own Exodus, with Bob as our leader.

Of course, at times it seemed like Bob had exchanged Kingston's Front Line for another, that of All Saints' Road, a short block away from the Basing Street studio and a centre for black activism. The studio was actually on the route of the West Indian Carnival, which had been

founded in the early 1960s but erupted into a war between black and white youth and the police just months before the Exodus sessions. Inevitably, despite the absence of bodyguards, the stress of the streets intruded at times. Early one Saturday evening, Angus 'Drummie' Gaye, Aswad's teenage drummer, came in seething because he'd just been arrested under the archaic 'sus' law, which had been designed to allow police to control vagrancy by apprehending people suspected of loitering with intent; it was now being widely used to harass young black males. Having been betrayed by his own island's 'politrickal' system, Bob could identify with the young musician. But soon Drummie was laughing again, as Bob would cry, 'Come on Aswad, me gonna mash up all a dem!' and the fussball game would defuse the tension. In this precious safe space, the making of *Exodus* was a defiant exorcism.

The broad arc of Exodus is an archetypal survival narrative so powerful that it seemed as if the album had sprung full-grown from Marley's head as a strategic, spiritual self-help manual on surviving conflict and betrayal and attaining happiness. Yet when these tracks were cut, there was no idea of the running order later selected from a cornucopia of material by Chris Blackwell and instantly approved by Bob and Family Man.

So, with no road map, the Wailers just kept on cutting, in a mood of exuberant creativity. As their engineer, Karl Pitterson, recalls, they were always well rehearsed and didn't like to leave the studio with work unfinished. A Wailers session was generally comfortable, with an atmosphere of relaxed discipline. All the musicians were masters, most of them trained by years of working in – actually, helping to create – the fiercely competitive world of Kingston recording sessions. It was normal to build, in a single take, a rhythm that still shakes the world, three decades on. The basic track was laid down by the Barrett brothers, bassist Family Man and drummer Carlton, with Tyrone Downie on piano and Bob himself providing the skank guitar that is reggae's trademark. Then came the extra layers of horns, backing vocals from the I-Threes, lead guitar from Junior Marvin, additional keyboards from Tyrone, percussion from Alvin 'Seeco' Patterson and others, and finally Bob's lead vocal.

Searching for the perfect intonation and inflection, locked in his own concentration, Bob would test each line this way and that, shifting the stress on a word or flipping the rhythm of his delivery, squeezing the juice from every line. This exploration took its own time but Bob never stopped experimenting, testing the tug of his voice with the rhythm, until he was satisfied.

Throughout the recording process he kept on writing songs: 'Exodus' itself came quite late, and has the sound of the whole Rasta family in its bones. There was a fizzing excitement around that track from the moment it was first laid down in the Fallout Shelter. All the assembled dreads rushed down the narrow stairs to the studio, eager to capture their urgency on wax. The song had so many meanings for them all, many of them exiles, virtually refugees themselves; and then of course there was an overriding Rasta concern, that of repatriation to Africa, which Bob was actively engaged in helping make real with the Twelve Tribes organization on land made available by Haile Selassie in Shashamane, Ethiopia. So the song's chorus features the voices of the whole powerful, dread-driven posse – all the Wailers, their art director, Neville Garrick, Satch, and King Sounds – all the bred'ren who were sharing the exile, a travelling family.

Bob was thinking a lot about movement back then. 'It's movement time!' he would cry when marshalling the troops. 'How you feel in life?' he asked me one night. 'You feel – movement?' When I affirmed, he nodded, 'Good.' Changes had to be made, Bob reasoned, and this was no time to stand still... The events of the day, including the struggle in South Africa and Rhodesia (which was shortly to become Zimbabwe), were frequently debated with the assembled bred'ren when Bob wasn't directly needed in the studio. Not surprisingly, he was usually quite scathing and cynical towards governments and the media. During one general reasoning about the corruption of our information sources, he flashed me a knowing look and said, quite sharply, 'Even if you wanted to write more 'bout Africa, (the editors) probably not gonna print it.'

And there was time to talk. Some mixes, like that of the blithely infectious 'Jamming', seemed to take forever as Blackwell and Pitterson debated specifics of the drum sound or the attack of the rhythm guitar, and the level of weed in the open bag on top of the desk steadily dropped. Restlessly, Bob would attack the fussball table, slamming the ball till it bounced between the plastic footballers, muttering, 'Energy low.'

But when the night came to finish 'Exodus' at Basing Street, the studio felt alive with excitement. There were plenty of original touches to the track – the pioneering use of the vocoder, for example, on the line 'movement of Jah people', an effect that wouldn't come into its own till the following decade – as well as Pitterson's idea of sprinkling a little disco groove on to Carly Barrett's drums. From the start, the track had its own impetus. Various pairs of hands – Family Man, Pitterson, Blackwell, sometimes even the young assistant engineers, Dick Cuthell and Terry Barham – all danced around and between each other on the mixing board faders, spontaneously and intuitively adjusting the levels to achieve ultimate dynamism. Every pass sounded superb, but at four o'clock in the morning a moment hit when the whole room knew that this one was it. 'Exodus' was militant and liberating, and as we all skanked and sang the chorus, Bob moved like the track was live-wiring his whole being. It seemed certain that

this song would mobilize millions, all of Jah people everywhere, to critique their existence and try to improve the world by any means possible.

When the time came to road-test the track, Basing Street proved a fine location. The area was dotted with shebeens, Jamaican after-hours joints that happened in abandoned buildings and basements, fire hazards all. Shebeens were the laboratory for the mid-1970s London sound that remains the basis of so much popular music and that Bob memorably called the 'punky reggae party'. The Clash, the Slits, the odd Sex Pistol, Chrissie Hynde and Boy George would skank there with reggae artists like Aswad and Steel Pulse, the great Alton Ellis or a visiting Dennis Brown and his producer, Niney. At the Metro Youth Club, right by the studio, when Matumbi's Dennis Bovell's Sufferers Sound played to celebrate His Imperial Majesty Haile Selassie's Birthday on July 23, 1977, Family Man showed up with a mix of 'Exodus'. The mostly school-age dancers – Britain's first homegrown Rasta generation, in red, green and gold tams and belts, the 'dawtas' in headwraps and knee-length skirts – started stepping as soon as needle hit wax. The song was speaking directly to them and every step brought them closer to the new consciousness they sought.

Bob appreciated those Metro excursions, but generally hung back in the shadows. He liked to watch how the people felt the music. And over the coming years he would have plenty of opportunity to observe dancers being galvanized by the head charge of *Exodus*. The album became a new milestone in his popularity and consolidated his position on the international music scene, effecting a transition in his life and career – an Exodus of his own existence whose direction took shape during winter months holed up in a couple of West London basement studios that somehow held the whole world.

Under the Westway, the flyover that carries the motorway above the houses and street markets of Notting Hill, sound system men prepare their equipment for the Carnival.

4 LIVING ON THE FRONT LINE

Living in London also gave Marley the added freedom of not having to deal with the sort of day-to-day hassles that came with taking his international success back home to Kingston. At that time he was exceptional as a Jamaican who had made it big yet hadn't moved up the hill – literally or metaphorically – to cut himself off from his previous life with high gates and attack dogs. The only way he would live his life was to keep his Hope Road yard as open as possible, to hang out on First Street down in Trenchtown and reason with the people, or to go running on the beach at Bull Bay, but such apparent accessibility came at a price. A price other than the obvious one of automatic weapons fire in the kitchen.

If a man under such improved circumstances as Marley's doesn't put the barriers up, the Jamaican people will assume an ownership, which involves 24-hour intellectual and critical access and full financial benefits. A Jamaican celebrity downtown is a bit like a cross between a Mafia don and a cash-point. The area's sufferahs have the right to share your wealth, to openly judge you or your work, to come to you with their

problems and woe betide you if you pretend not to notice them. While any compassionate person would want to do what they could for those less fortunate, in Kingston the sheer volume of demands could threaten to overwhelm and

distract someone such as Marley from his work and the things he had to do to be in a position to help the needy. In England he remained hugely generous to the people back home and to more than a few in London, but it made considerable difference to be removed from the frequently exhausting and seemingly unending demands of his former peers.

The new environment, however, wasn't totally removed from how things were done in sufferahs' Jamaica. Which was wholly intentional. While holed up in a Nassau villa belonging to Chris Blackwell after the Smile Jamaica concert, the Wailers party,

which included Bob, the musicians, the I-Threes, the art director Neville Garrick and the road manager Allan 'Skill' Cole, held long discussions about where they should set up home. Cuba was near the top of the agenda, largely because Fidel Castro, who was close to Michael Manley, had invited them and the climate would be so similar to Jamaica's – this was January, and Marley's last winter in the UK had

> IN ENGLAND HE REMAINED HUGELY GENEROUS TO THE PEOPLE BACK HOME AND TO MORE THAN A FEW IN LONDON, BUT IT MADE A CONSIDERABLE DIFFERENCE TO BE REMOVED FROM THE FREQUENTLY EXHAUSTING AND SEEMINGLY UNENDING DEMANDS OF HIS FORMER PEERS

© Kate Simon

Above: In his adopted home by the Thames, Marley is flanked by two members of the band of Rico Rodrigues, who provided the horn section for the Exodus tour.

Opposite: Movement of Jah people as Marley, Tyrone Downie and Family Man Barrett take to two wheels.

yet to be forgotten. Cuba was subsequently turned down for a number of reasons. Marley didn't want anybody's political agenda becoming attached to his move, particularly after the way Smile Jamaica had been hijacked, and the group were agreed this would be unavoidable if they moved to Cuba. Plus he was well aware that being a guest of the CIA's then Public Enemy No 1 would not have been the smartest move for an artist making serious inroads into the American market. And there was the potential problem of a sustainable supply of high-grade collie weed on an island with virtually no ganja trade, and a government that couldn't be seen to be sanctioning open drug use from official guests.

If they weren't going to remain in the Caribbean then London was the obvious choice, and not simply because it made the most practical sense. London had reliable communications and transport links, the group would have access to the required level of recording facilities (which didn't exist in Nassau at that time), and their record company, Island, had its head office there. But the UK capital also had a large and vibrant Jamaican community, and from his previous visits Marley was well aware that, culturally speaking, London would be the closest thing to a home away from home outside parts of Queens in New York. Food from Jamaica would be as readily available as

the local news, and there would be a guaranteed supply of herb. There was an established Twelve Tribes organization in London which could provide a spiritual base for the devout Rastas and a calm and trustworthy 'in' into unseen black London. Most important, there was the notion that they could associate and surround themselves with people they knew how to talk to and behave around, enormously easing the group's transition to a new environment.

This was no mere convenience; it was a necessity, given that they were still vividly reliving the experience of having a posse of gunmen invade their home. Psychological security was of greater concern than physical security at this point, and it was absolutely vital that the party felt safe as opposed to simply being safe. Hearing Jamaican voices and eating Jamaican food would be as comforting to them as Britain's rigid firearms laws, which, in 1977, still counted for something. The sight of dreadlocks had become common enough on London's streets not to attract attention – other than, perhaps, from vindictive policemen or store detectives with nothing better to do. After what had gone down in Kingston the Wailers wanted nothing more than to live a low-key existence, and the ability to disappear into the city's Jamaican community without attracting any attention

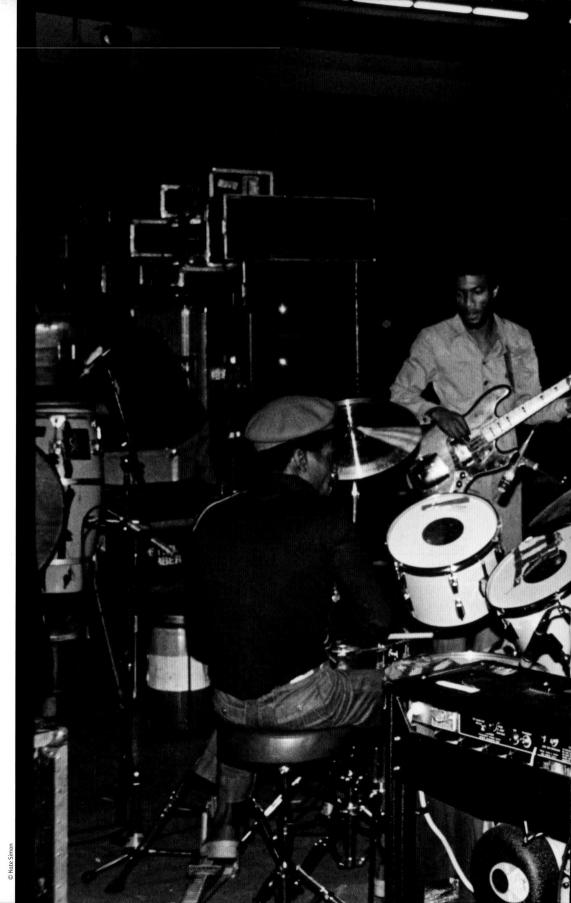

Many of the songs from *Exodus* became staples of the Wailers' live shows. Here they are at a sound check, from left: Carlton Barrett, Tyrone Downie (temporarily abandoning his keyboards for a bass guitar), Family Man Barrett, Marley and Junior Marvin.

suited them perfectly. This was particularly useful to Marley himself, as he had been elevated from the British music press favourite he'd become after the Lyceum show in 1975, to a British tabloid staple due to their editors' fascination with his sex life, his ganja consumption and his dreadlocks. When it became known he and Cindy Breakspeare, a Jamaican woman recently crowned Miss World, were now an item, the tabloids' showbiz reporters went into 'Beauty And The Beast' headline overkill. Remarkably, the Wailers' quest for privacy worked so well, and Chris Blackwell's office kept the secret so securely, that nobody even knew they were in London for the first couple of months of their stay. Their anonymity only came to an end when Neville Garrick and Carlton Barrett were out food-shopping in Shepherds Bush Market and bumped into the music journalist Vivien Goldman, who knew them well from the times she had been out to Jamaica to do stories on the group. But even after she had outed their arrival in London, they still managed to live the private life they sought.

In total control of their environment, the Wailers were able spend the first few weeks in England re-establishing a collective peace of mind and allowing the wounds – physical and psychological – to heal without pressure from the local reggae crowd or from well-meaning associates. And although there was very little writing or recording done during those early days, their new London address had its own positive effect on the music they would be making.

© Kate Simon

MARLEY WAS ALMOST FANATICAL ABOUT MAKING MUSIC VIA A GROUP MENTALITY, AND ALTHOUGH HE WAS ALWAYS GOING TO BE THE FRONT MAN AND THE FOCAL POINT IN EVERY RESPECT, HE KNEW THAT IF HE GOT THE PERSONNEL RIGHT, IN TERMS OF PERSONALITIES AS WELL AS ABILITIES, A GOOD GROUP WOULD ALWAYS BE STRONGER THAN THE SUM OF ITS PARTS

The Wailers were installed in a large four-storey terrace house in Oakley Street, an upmarket road running between the King's Road, Chelsea, and the north end of Albert Bridge, which spans the River Thames. Each man had his own room, meaning that instruments, tape recorders and Family Man's array of high-tech studio gadgetry were all easily accommodated, and the musicians could work up their own ideas in relative privacy, but with the others on hand for consultation if needed. The large kitchen/dining room served as a communal hangout, and was where for the first couple of months Neville Garrick and Carly Barrett did the cooking, until former Christine Keeler associate Lucky Gordon was taken on as in-house chef. A prominent feature of this room was the television, which would become a focus of boisterous attention any time there was a football match showing.

This is hardly surprising, since football had assumed an almost transcendental status in Marley's life. The proximity of the house at 52 Oakley Street to Battersea Park – which lay just the other side of Albert Bridge – was the main reason it was selected. Quickly, the days took on a straightforward routine: get up around lunchtime; play football in the park; rest up and eat; leave to go to the studio or to rehearsal late evening; return in the early hours; get up around lunchtime...

On the surface it was little different from how they might have structured things in Jamaica if they were recording an album, but as far as Marley was concerned their UK situation held one massive advantage: everybody was together, all the time. He would frequently talk about his musicians and other personnel as being family, and now they could actually live like one. He had always looked forward to touring because being on the road meant that everybody was living together, exchanging ideas and contributing musically and intellectually to the group's development. When they came off the road, however, everybody scattered to their own homes and separate lives and the group dynamic would be temporarily lost.

Marley was almost fanatical about making music via a group mentality, and although he was always going to be the front man and the focal point in every respect, he knew that if he got the personnel right, in terms of personalities as well as abilities, a good group would always be stronger than the sum of its parts. This was highly unusual, perhaps unique, in the Jamaican music business – where, even as late as 1977, it was as if the Beatles had never happened. The studio system of producers cutting songs on singers with the same house band for everybody had even translated to the live experience, where

singers invariably used pick-up bands provided by the promoter or their producer, meaning there was seldom any creative interplay beyond accurately reproducing the singles on stage. When the Wailers were still a vocal trio they recruited the Barrett brothers out of Lee Perry's Upsetters to be their permanent rhythm section, and from then on Marley wanted to take the idea of a genuine reggae group to its furthest creative point, both in the studio and on stage. He believed a collective lifestyle was vital to the collective musical effort, and in London he relished the opportunity to make it work. It would be difficult to argue against his theories, too, given the cohesion, continuity and detailed exploration of themes on both *Exodus* and *Kaya*.

The idea was to create what might be described as a gang mentality, and the Oakley Street Boys' Club – football, music, shared food, chalices, meandering reasoning sessions – fulfilled this bonding brief perfectly. With Rita Marley and the other two I-Threes, Judy Mowatt and Marcia Griffiths, installed in an apartment about a mile away in Earl's Court, the manly environment could be preserved. Socially progressive as Bob Marley might have been, he was still (a) Jamaican and (b) a Rasta, therefore a male-oriented situation was pretty much how things should be. Of course

© Kate Simon

Marley was the front man, the one who drew the attention and the headlines, but he always believed that the music flowed most effectively when the musicians lived and worked together, as they did during the period that produced *Exodus*. When the album was finished, a tour of Europe and the UK maintained the feeling of a creative unit.

this arrangement was useful in other respects. Rita was close enough for him to take round his washing and ironing for her to take care of, but far enough removed to turn a blind eye to her husband's serial philandering.

Bob Marley's serious squeeze at the time was Cindy Breakspeare, who was based in London to carry out her Miss World duties for that year. She had flown to Nassau to be with him, and now they would spend time together at Oakley Street or in some of the capital's more discreet hotels. Other dalliances included a member of the Libyan royal family and an Ethiopian princess descended from Haile Selassie, but it was Breakspeare who made Marley happiest. People close to them at the time have frequently described the pair as soul mates, and the situation of being relaxed and comfortable and able to spend time with a woman he was smitten with contributed greatly to love songs like 'Waiting in Vain' and 'Turn Your Lights Down Low' on *Exodus* and enabled *Kaya* to be the smoothest, most joyfully contented collection of songs the Wailers ever put together.

Football came a close second to music in the house on Oakley Street, where the Wailers could relax in the knowledge that their daily needs would be provided for. The veil of secrecy drawn over their arrival in London meant that they could lead a comparatively unhassled existence.

© Kate Simon

THE FOOTBALL MATCH

RICHARD WILLIAMS

Football was not in the least fashionable in the England of the mid-1970s. By and large, it was still what it had always been: the winter game of the working class, played in dilapidated stadiums on pitches often turned into quagmires by rain or snow. England's national team had not qualified for the 1974 World Cup finals, and would repeat the failure four years later. Manchester United were in the doldrums, Chelsea were in the old Second Division, and their players were very far from being millionaires. Hooliganism, closely associated with the skinhead cult, was still a major issue. But Bob Marley loved football of a different kind, and he brought that love of a sun-splashed game with him when he arrived in London in the early weeks of 1977.

When it came to football, Marley was one of nature's Brazilians. He loved the vision, the close ball-control, the outrageous feats of the imagination and the technical tricks patented by the 1970 world champions – Pelé, Jairzino, Gerson, Tostão, Roberto Rivelino and their team mates. Among his closest friends was Allan Cole, then Jamaica's best-known player, a fellow Rastafarian whose nickname was 'Skill'.

'Bob was football,' Al Anderson, one of the Wailers' guitarists at the time of *Exodus*, said in *Rebel Music*, a Channel 4/WNET documentary on Marley's life. 'That was his chess game – scoring and dodging and faking out and making the move. He wanted to win everything.'

'He was passionate about football,' Cindy Breakspeare, his girlfriend during the Exodus year, told the same programme. 'Anywhere they went, they would get a match together.' Before Marley had been in England long he had let the people around him know that he would not

Marley played football everywhere he could, and one day early in the early weeks of 1977 the Wailers' team took on their opponents from Island Records on a pitch in Battersea Park. Marley is flanked in the photograph by the art director Neville Garrick (left) and his cook and minder Antonio "Gilly" Gilbert (right). Twenty two years later Jamaica's football squad, nicknamed the Reggae Boyz, would qualify for the finals of the World Cup.

be averse to taking part in a game, and one was duly organised between a Wailers XI and a team drawn from the staff of Island Records. Skill Cole was not around but Bob was joined by Antonio 'Gilly' Gilbert, whose multiple roles in his entourage encompassed those of friend, travelling chef and designated minder on the football pitch. Wearing a blue track suit and with his locks gathered inside a striped woolly hat, Bob quickly showed his English opponents the evidence of a technique developed playing in the yards and on the beaches of his boyhood.

'They were so good it was like playing Brazil,' remembered Trevor Wyatt, a member of the Island staff who organised the match on a pitch in Battersea Park, on the south bank of the Thames. 'Bob had all the skills. Once he had the ball, you could never get it off him.'

'In fact you weren't allowed to get it off him,' added John Knowles, then a member of Island's sales force and more recently the manager of the singer Chris Rea. 'If you did, Gilly would just tread all over you. Bob was a fantastic player. He played up front – centre forward, anywhere he could score. He had great ball skills – balancing the ball on his boot, that sort of thing. And he was very quick, too. He never headed the ball, obviously, because the tea cosy would have fallen off.' Knowles had one particularly vivid memory: 'I remember him leaning on the goalpost after he'd scored, smoking a spliff.'

Marley's love of football was to have fateful consequences. Some time earlier, during a game in Trenchtown, he had injured his big toe, which went black under the nail. When the Exodus tour reached Paris, he took part in another impromptu match and a challenge from an opposing player exacerbated the injury. This time it was bandaged up, and he thought little of it until its condition gradually worsened to the point where treatment was necessary.

'He wouldn't give it a chance to heal,' Cindy Breakspeare remembered, but eventually, on July 7, 1977, soon after the four London concerts that marked the end of the European leg of the Exodus tour, he was persuaded to submit to a medical examination by a Harley Street consultant. 'And that was when they detected the melanoma, the skin cancer,' Breakspeare continued. 'They removed the actual nail, and the nail bed, and they did a graft from his leg over it so there was no toe nail at all there.'

The diagnosis caused the immediate cancellation of plans to extend the tour to the United States. But it was not until the autumn of 1980, during a subsequent American tour, that Bob collapsed while jogging in New York's Central Park and was told that the cancer had made its fatal progress to his brain.

THE IDEA WAS TO CREATE WHAT MIGHT BE DESCRIBED
AS A GANG MENTALITY, AND THE OAKLEY STREET BOYS'
CLUB – FOOTBALL, MUSIC, SHARED FOOD, CHALICES,
MEANDERING REASONING SESSIONS – FULFILLED THIS
BONDING BRIEF PERFECTLY

If everyone who claimed to have attended the Lyceum concerts on July 17 and 18, 1975 had been telling the truth, Marley would have been watched by more people than the FA Cup final. As it was, so many people managed to get in that the old theatre's retractable roof had to be opened to provide ventilation for the packed crowd, who revelled in the music's sweltering heat.

IN BRITAIN IN 1977, THE MAINSTREAM MUSIC INDUSTRY OFFERED THE SORT OF SCOPE A MAN LIKE MARLEY NEEDED, ALTHOUGH THIS WAS MORE BY DEFAULT THAN BY DESIGN

5 THE PUNKY REGGAE PARTY

Musically, London in 1977 was the coolest place for a band like the Wailers to be. The *Exodus/Kaya* sessions were the first time this modern incarnation of Bob Marley had recorded outside Jamaica. Anywhere other than Kingston at that time would have been a leap forward for an artist with Marley's vision, but here was the perfect artistic environment in which to create songs with such breadth and depth.

The way the studio system worked in Kingston in 1977 was much the same as had been in 1967 and, for that matter, how it remains in 2007 – producers paired singers with backing tracks that were either played live or pre-recorded, to provide a rhythm for lyrics the singer might have written for himself, or maybe the producer provided for him. As the copyright laws were still years away from being applied to music in Jamaica, owner-ship of a song rested with the ownership of that particular recording, so plagiarism and copying

were rife. If a producer wanted to 'version' (cover) a rival's hit tune, he would simply employ the same musicians to play it in his studio, then get one of his singers to supply his own vocals. The public who bought the records and attended the sound systems had no problems with any of this, and since new versions of recent tunes enjoyed all the standing of a new song, this famously meant some popular rhythms were versioned over a hundred times.

Although Marley had the clout, the wherewithal and the sense of his own destiny not to subscribe to this way of doing things, on an island as small as Jamaica, in a situation as claustrophobic as the Kingston music business, it would be impossible to remain untouched by such methods. Its creeping influence would be as a parallel with the perpetual pressures of Marley's everyday life in that city, and it would have been impossible for him and his group not to be swayed into making unconscious compromises with the industry around them – not least because Bob Marley was the consummate diplomat, and therefore would have been obliged

to present a certain face at home. And while that is probably a good thing if you want to pander to a reggae audience, for anybody with a rock star ambition it was far too inward-looking.

London far better suited his aspirations. Studios were simply rooms where artists recorded songs, rather than a step back into feudal times; producers were there to facilitate the music; and recording as a group was the norm – even in the reggae business. By physically removing himself from every aspect of Kingston's way of doing things, the Exodus/Kaya recording sessions were relaxed enough to reveal Bob Marley's personality rather than simply a mixture of his personae.

In Britain in 1977, the mainstream music industry offered the sort of scope a man like Marley needed, although this was more by default than by design. There were very few radio stations, they weren't formatted and most shows played what was in the Top 40. And because the charts were compiled by record sales rather than airplay, pop radio and TV programmes would feature some scarcely believable mix-ups of music – it would not be unusual to find a Top 20 featuring country and western, reggae, disco, straight pop, progressive rock, with the Sex Pistols, Acker Bilk and the Muppets all getting airplay on the same BBC Radio One daytime shows (well, maybe not the Sex Pistols). And because cassette players were still a pricey optional extra in cars, most car radios would be tuned to the BBC, so those wanting an eclectic soundtrack to their lives would find it virtually impossible from the moment they left their house. The live rock scene in the capital had never been healthier. As a reaction to prog rock's towering, distancing pomposity and glam rock's appeal to a younger audience, it seemed that everybody was forming a band. By 1977 it was virtually impossible to have a quiet drink in a London pub without a bunch of musicians setting up in the corner to blast the customers with an hour of R&B. It was an exciting time, opening up all sorts of venues, getting fans out to sweaty gigs again, and producing a wave of bands with splendidly broad-based repertoires. Ian Dury and the Blockheads, Elvis Costello and the Attractions, the Police, Dr Feelgood and Eddie and the Hotrods all came out of this scene, while the same circuit allowed the punk movement to grow by giving those groups somewhere to perform before any of them had made records.

Even if a group of musicians like the Wailers ventured no further than the London reggae scene, it would have been difficult for them not to have their horizons broadened. As a by-product of London's Jamaican community, over a period of 20 years the city had developed a thriving sound system scene, originally run along Jamaican lines and relying on the uniqueness of imported specials to decide operators' rankings. By 1977, however, a home-grown reggae scene was booming as second-generation black kids were coming into it to make, perform and deejay their own sounds and were starting to shape the music into something that better met their needs. After all, significant numbers had no Jamaican heritage, so why adhere rigidly to the Kingston model?

The main difference was that British youngsters formed groups, because that was how things

were done in the UK music industry – Steel Pulse, Aswad, Matumbi, and Misty in Roots were among those making waves. And UK reggae had a different tone. Although the musicians were steeped in Jamaican roots reggae – quite rightly feeling that the sentiments could be applied to their own situation – they had grown up listening to a much broader range of music, and would therefore always have a different sensibility. Plus what most of their music would be aiming at was not the same as a made-in-Jamaica record: because there were fewer independent record companies at that time, and the reggae industry could not sustain itself, the bands looked to sign with major labels, which meant their records needed one eye on the pop mainstream. It resulted in reggae that was written and played by groups with a pop/rock awareness but who were determined not to compromise their core values, would deal with social issues and could perform live on stage.

Since 1975 there had also been a huge lovers' rock scene in the UK. It couldn't have been further from roots reggae, with lyrics specialised in young love and all its attendant joys and despairs, while the easy-action music reflected a teenage audience well-versed in Philly soul, Motown, funk and pop, then served it up with a reggae beat. But with its own sound systems, record labels and underground superstars, lovers' rock had grown to such a degree that it was influencing Jamaican reggae, as artists came over and immersed themselves in it before taking ideas home.

That London as a musical environment hugely influenced the Wailers as they recorded the tunes that would become *Exodus* and *Kaya* is without question. Just being out and about or turning the radio on would have underlined the fact that, at that time, mainstream tastes were far more adventurous than might have been imagined. Or that a left-field genre, e.g. reggae, could be accepted as a bona fide element of rock, provided it made the necessary concessions to that audience's preferences. Or that reggae played by groups stands a much better chance via live performance, and, as their Lyceum success had taught the Wailers, live work was the key to sustained rock success. Or that, and this would have been important, provided it was clever enough, reggae could take on board the influences it required to help it cross over without compromising the notion that it remained reggae first and foremost.

Steel Pulse ticked many of these boxes, and so impressed members of the Wailers they nagged Island Records into signing the group during the summer of 1977. Then they took the Birmingham rootsmen to open for them on the first leg of the

Exodus tour. It surprised many close observers of the Wailers in London that they hadn't opted for Aswad as their support, since the members of that young West London group – also signed to Island – hung out with them in the studios and would regularly be involved in marathon table football games with Marley himself. But their reasons for picking Pulse said a great deal about the Wailers' approach to reggae. They believed that group had a much broader, more progressive and authentically British sound, whereas Aswad simply wanted to be Bob Marley and the Wailers.

The general absorption of influences from their host city was also a ringing endorsement of Marley's belief in the group mentality. It wasn't Marley himself who picked up this extraneous stuff; it was the musicians who worked up their own takes on what they had heard, then played it back to the Skipper. Marley came up with the melodies, always the greatest strength of the Wailers' material and the reason their stuff was so mainstream-friendly, but the others brought the embellishments that made the tunes truly special. Marley rarely left the house unless to play

Even a hotel room provided a place
to practise football skills.
From left: Neville Garrick (in Exodus
tour T-shirt), Gilly, Alvin 'Seeco'
Patterson and Marley.

football, to go the studio or to keep a lovers' tryst somewhere. He preferred to hold court rather than hang out, receiving visitors in his rooms at Oakley Street. Maybe it was lingering worries about safety that stopped him going to sound system dances in London, but that doesn't account for the fact that whenever he was being driven anywhere in one of the cars the others had hired, the first thing he would do was turn the radio off. He didn't play other artists' records and would only pay attention to *Top of the Pops* if there was a chance one of their records was going to chart. It was one of the most unexpected things about Bob Marley: open-minded as he appeared to be, he rarely listened to music other than his own.

Neville Garrick, Family Man Barrett and Tyrone Downie were the most active conduits to the London music scene. Family Man loved music across the board and would go to gigs, spend hours in record shops and avail himself of the capital's night clubs. Garrick and Downie were less adventurous but, in the company of Trevor Bow of the local group Sons of Jah, they threw themselves in to London's reggae world with considerable gusto. As well as checking out the bands – favourites were Steel Pulse and Matumbi – they were regulars at Lloydie Coxsone's Sunday night sessions at the Four Aces club in Dalston and often dropped in on Dennis Bovell's Sufferer HiFi at the Metro in Ladbroke Grove. Both soundmen would spin selections of their own UK-produced lovers' rock and imaginative dubs alongside the imported JA specials and it was these different sounds that particularly caught the visitors' attention.

HE DIDN'T PLAY OTHER ARTISTS' RECORDS AND WOULD ONLY PAY ATTENTION TO *TOP OF THE POPS* IF THERE WAS A CHANCE ONE OF THEIR RECORDS WAS GOING TO CHART

To a devout Rasta, ganja represents a sacrament validated by the words of the Bible. A favourite reference came from the Book of Psalms: 'He that causeth the grass to grow for the cattle, and herb for the service of man, that he may bring forth food out of the world.' Marley felt that ganja encouraged the contemplatation of spiritual values and saw in the herb 'the healing of a nation'. Later, some observers would attempt to blame it for the spread of his cancer.

When the Wailers signed to Island, Chris Blackwell believed that if they were given the same treatment as a rock group, they might attain a similar level of acceptance. Promoted via posters on the sides of London buses, they were given the kind of tour support that rock musicians had come to see as theirs by right but which was completely new to reggae. The strategy achieved a degree of success far beyond Blackwell's dreams.

> MARLEY DEMANDED A SIMILARLY SERIOUS APPROACH FROM THE MUSICIANS, WITH CONSTANT LATE-NIGHT REHEARSALS TO IRON OUT GLITCHES AND A DISCIPLINED APPROACH TO TIME-KEEPING AND BEHAVIOUR

6 TAKING IT TO THE WORLD

With all those influences and all that energy going into it, it is hardly surprising *Exodus* was a huge success: Top 10 in the UK, where the group finished the year as the country's ninth best-selling albums group (above Yes, and below Queen), and Top 20 in the US. But then it had as much going for it after it was released as it had had while it was being made.

The album had enjoyed promotion on an unprecedented scale for a reggae act – the giant posters on London buses and in Underground stations prompted group members to remark it was just like being in a big-time rock group. Which was exactly how Chris Blackwell saw Bob Marley and The Wailers in 1977, not as a reggae act like their labelmates Max Romeo or Burning Spear. And because he didn't have to clear it with anybody else, he could assign an appropriate marketing budget.

Blackwell was equally shrewd over the album's track selection. The London sessions had produced a couple of dozen songs spanning a spectrum of Marley's moods since leaving Jamaica, from righteous fury to bliss. It had long since been decided to put together two albums, but it was

much later in the process, after all the finished tracks had been assembled, that the label boss opted to divide them according to two major facets of Marley's personality: the revolutionary and the romantic. Hence *Exodus's* more strident, politically charged emphasis and *Kaya's* concentration on gentler love songs. He also took the unexpected step of releasing the militant collection first, before following it less than a year later with the softer, more pop-friendly set. With an artist as seemingly unconventional as Bob Marley, in their first real big marketing push, most companies would have done it the other way around, seducing the newcomer with the love songs and then, once they were hooked, hitting them with the rebel music. But Blackwell reckoned socio-political was what Bob Marley did, and as this clutch of songs was less traditionally roots 'n' culture and more relevant to the global situation, this is what he should come with first. He wanted people to get their heads round that first, then, almost by way of reward, they could chill out a bit with their kaya and some easy-action, loose-limbed skanking.

The tour around Europe that summer was also approached as a serious rock-style venture, with a budget to match; and it worked wonders for the

group. The high levels of comfort and equipment were unknown among reggae acts back then, and Marley demanded a similarly serious approach from the musicians, with constant late-night rehearsals to iron out glitches and a disciplined approach to timekeeping and behaviour. What pleased the whole party most was that they were able to present what they did in its entire glory. Neville Garrick's fabulous hand-painted Rasta-themed stage backdrops set the show's tone and introduced audiences to the band's beliefs. Red, green and gold lighting, again designed by Garrrick, carried this through and raised the energy levels with its sense of drama and movement. And the big stages made room for Marley – dancing, leaping, brooding and posing like a true superstar – to give some of the finest shows of his career.

The toe injury which forced the cancellation of plans to take the show across the Atlantic that summer, after the completion of the European dates, denied Marley the opportunity to lay waste to US audiences. By that point, however, he had a ready-made rock audience in the UK, Europe and the US, who ate up the socio-politics with a stick. This following had first been noticed in the

At the Rainbow theatre on June 4, 1977, Bob Marley and the Wailers played for the last time in front of the spectacular stage backdrop for the *Exodus* shows: a portrait of Ras Tafari himself, the Emperor Haile Selassie I of Ethiopia, hand-painted on canvas by Neville Garrick. In the *New York Times Magazine*, the journalist Jon Bradshaw described the atmosphere: 'So he comes jiggling out on to the stage, this wiry, spindle-shanked singer, this self-styled black prince of reggae, his clenched fist high above his head, his dreadlocks flopping round his ears. The crowd rises to its feet and begins to scream and the singer shouts, "Yes!" and the crowd shouts "Yes! Yes! Yes!" And then, with slight menace in his voice, the singer says, "Jesu, light the fire to my salvation. Whom shall I fear? Jah. Ras Tafari." And the crowd screams 'Jah, Jah, Ras Tafari' and begins to whistle and clap and the band begins to play and the singer slides into one of his early songs called "Lively Up Yourself"… On the stage behind Marley is a lurid backdrop, complete with huts, fires and telegraph poles – meant to resemble Trenchtown, the squalid Kingston ghetto where he was raised. To the right of the stage is a flag of Ethiopia and a banner depicting the Conquering Lion of Judah. At Marley's previous London concert, there were numerous stabbings and tonight the police and vigilant groups of black security men prowl through the theatre. It is a young audience and the kids have taken to turning up at Marley's concerts in natty urban-guerrilla gear. Boots, berets and clenched-fist salutes are popular. The theatre is thick with the sharp aroma of burning marijuana… Marley breaks into "War", a speech of Haile Selassie's he set to music. It is like an invocation. "Until the philosophy which holds one race superior and another inferior is finally and permanently discredited and abandoned, everywhere is war. Me say war," he chants. Behind Marley the five Wailers strike up and, to the side, the I-Threes, Marley's backing singers in tribal dress, turbans and beaded necklaces, pick up the harmonies. Marley tends to act out his songs with exaggerated rage and anguish, throwing his head into his hands, crying or strutting up and down the stage. "Until the colour of a man's skin is of no more significance than the colour of his eyes, there will be war, everywhere war," he sings and all these clean and fresh-faced kids who wouldn't know the difference between an Ingram M10 and a machete scream and throw their fists in the air…'

Neville Garrick's backdrop is now on display in the Marley museum at 56 Hope Road.

Above: In Europe and the UK, audiences who had not seen him before were left in no doubt that Marley was among the most compelling performers of his time, with a stage presence that few could match.

Right: Seeco carries his ghetto-blaster – the iPod of the 1970s – through an airport terminal while Marley studies the *Daily Express*, his sandalled feet revealing the bandage on his right big toe.

By the time of *Exodus*, Rita Marley
was no longer living as Bob's wife.
They remained close, however, and
she continued to tour as a member
of the I-Threes.

Opposite: The tour ended in London
with four triumphant nights at the
old Finsbury Park Astoria, renamed
the Rainbow, where Marley sang in
front of Garrick's backcloth for
the last time.

Left: The boys on the bus; Marley and Gilly at rest.

Opposite, top: Clockwise from bottom left: Seeco Patterson, Junior Marvin, Neville Garrick, Marley, Tyrone Downie and Family Man Barrett.

Oppostite, bottom: Seeco, Marley and Family Man.

Bob, Gilly and Seeco, who is reading *People of Kau*, a photographic study of the people of south-east Nuba by Leni Riefenstahl, whose portraits of athletes at the 1936 Olympic Games made her famous.

Opposite: Marley warms up backstage for a show in Germany during the Exodus tour.

The Wailers had toured the United States to promote earlier albums, but plans for dates coinciding with the release of *Exodus* had to be cancelled when Marley's illness was diagnosed at the end of the series of European concerts. Nevertheless, the more eclectic approach of the new album won airplay, if not unanimous critical acclaim.

audience at the Lyceum gig two years earlier, and by 1977 and the release of *Exodus*, Marley and the Wailers had become the hippies' house band.

Even at that late date there were still plenty of hippies of all ages in circulation. But while their values and their ideology were still intact, their music had all but disappeared once the Los Angeles folk-rock scene reinvented itself as the Eagles. Acts such as the Byrds, James Taylor, and Crosby Stills, Nash and Young had left a large international audience primed for meaningful lyrics, easy melodies, lashings of spirituality and a mellow, spliff-driven vibe; but glam rock was pointless, soul was turning to disco, heavy metal took all the wrong drugs and prog's embrace of electronic technology and empty musical melodrama held no appeal. Bob Marley was absolutely tailor-made for this audience, and an LP like *Exodus* was always going to have a much better rhythm section than, say, Neil Young's latest effort if you fancied a bit of a dance. When the UK tour reached the Rainbow Theatre – the old Finsbury Park Astoria

– it became obvious that Marley had succeeded in his quest to take his roots sensibility to the mainstream, and that a largely white, middle-class audience had joyously bought into his message. It was no coincidence that Marley's big US break-through came in college radio and in California.

In the UK he also acquired something of a bonus audience, thanks to the so-called alliance between reggae and punk, a youth movement for disaffected white kids. The early council-estate punks bought roots reggae records for a number of reasons. First, they had black mates. Second, they found the sentiments gave voice to their own sense of frustration. Third, its ganja associations were always worthwhile. And fourth, heavy dub or toasting was probably the most obnoxious sounding noise their mums and dads had ever encountered. Big Youth was a favourite, as were Prince Far-I, Dillinger, Culture and anything with King Tubby's name on it. Whatever the original motives, however, by 1977 the Sex Pistols had sworn on live TV, the Stranglers were hit parade regulars

and punk had gone Top Shop. It had a uniform, a range of accessories and a prescribed set of values and responses, which still included a liking for reggae. Bob Marley and the Wailers, being the most accessible reggae band on the planet, were the biggest beneficiaries. Marley himself responded by celebrating his new acolytes with the single 'Punky Reggae Party', recorded with members of Aswad and Third World, produced by Lee Perry. If anybody else had made such a record they would have been accused of all manner of cynicism, but Marley's standing meant that the genuineness of his intentions was never doubted.

Every Wailers line-up had its own strengths, but this was a particularly well-favoured outfit: from left, Tyrone Downie, Family Man Barrett, Seeco Patterson, Carlton Barrett, Marley and Junior Marvin at a sound check.

© Kate Simon

The tour covered six countries in 13 nights. It began on May 10 in Paris, in a hall said to have once been a slaughterhouse, and continued through Brussels, The Hague, Munich, Heidelberg, Hamburg, Berlin (where they played in an ice stadium), Gothenburg, Stockholm and Copenhagen. Now the audiences included socialites in the VIP seats as well as hard-core reggae fans. In effect, the Wailers had become to the 1970s what the Rolling Stones were to the preceding decade: purveyors of rebel music with a hint of exoticism and an appeal that crossed all lines of class and geography.

THE BIG STAGES MADE ROOM FOR MARLEY – DANCING, LEAPING, BROODING AND POSING LIKE A TRUE SUPERSTAR

After closing the Continental leg
of the tour, the Wailers returned
to London and took a week off
before beginning their only
British dates: a four-night run
at the Rainbow from June 1-4,
where 80 security men and a
posse of uniformed police were
present every night to ensure
that there was no repeat of the
near-riots that had accompanied
the shows at Hammersmith
Odeon a year earlier.

STATESIDE SUFFERATION

ROBERT CHRISTGAU

England was ready for reggae because Jamaicans dominated Britain's black population. In the United States, only native-born African-Americans made the distinction, which they saw as invidious, between themselves and Jamaicans. As whites' awareness increased, it was striving Jamaican Baptists they noticed, church-proper with an English overlay in non-commercial jobs – nurses, transit personnel, museum guards. But Chris Blackwell changed that when he decided to make Bob Marley a rock star. Financing junket after junket, he supplanted the Jamaican Tourist Board and its Negril fantasies as the chief US source of Jamaican imagery. Tipping the balance was 'The Wild Side of Paradise', a mammoth July, 1973, *Rolling Stone* cover story by Australian-gone-native writer Michael Thomas, which kicked off the magazine's impressive 1970s reggae coverage. For a growing number of white Americans, the island came to seem the last great haven of long hair and marijuana – and of a musical ethos that honored the spiritual-political potential conceived for rock in hippie's heyday.

I was sent to Jamaica in 1973 myself – even shared a spliff while Marley unrolled some patois out in front of 56 Hope Road. But I resisted Blackwell's hype, championing Toots Hibbert because he channeled Otis Redding and interviewing Big Youth against the advice of Jamaican hipsters, certain he'd be soon gone. I'm glad I got one right. But I was hardly the only US journalist to doubt Marley. In the *Village Voice's* nationwide Pazz & Jop Critics' Poll, Natty Dread finished ninth in 1975 (Toots was thirteenth), whereupon Marley's critical fortunes sank – *Live!* squeaked in the same year *Rastaman Vibration* didn't, and after that his only finisher was 1979's *Survival*.

With Marley canonized and his songs worn so deep into our memories that they seem as natural as the birds and the fishes, these judgments play poorly today. Note, however, that had the poll existed in 1972 and 1973, the critics would have backed Catch a Fire and especially Burnin'. Though Blackwell disparages Burnin' – 'its cohesiveness, its sound, even the playing,' he told Vivien Goldman – it's as classic as Exodus. It's the most basic music Marley ever recorded for Island, as well as his toughest and catchiest collection of songs. Nor were they all his – Burnin' is a full-fledged Wailers record, topping the deeply funky Barrett brothers with natural militant Peter Tosh and

natural mystic Bunny Livingston. Many early American Wailers fans never forgot or altogether forgave the loss of those two independent creative forces. Yet though the I-Threes were always a tad too girly for the rock utopians who hoped reggae was the second coming, they dug Natty Dread nevertheless.

The deal-breaker was *Rastaman Vibration*, and one reason can't be denied: as songwriting, it's a step down, with 'Positive Vibration' and 'Roots, Rock, Reggae' among the flattest of Marley's many attempts to cosset the rock audience. That's why critics turned to the rough-hewn *Live!*, which from the opening lines of the US-unavailable 'Trenchtown Rock' hit you and felt all right. But the audience got cosseted anyway. *Rastaman Vibration* was the only Marley album to go Top 10 stateside, behind FM play for 'Roots, Rock, Reggae' and a tour of midsize venues like Boston's Music Hall, New York's Beacon and Oakland's Paramount. In *Rolling Stone*, the late Robert Palmer leaned over backwards to praise the album – Marley's genius was precisely to his disruptive, R&B-rooted, Afro-internationalist taste. But his praise didn't extend to what he called 'the mushrooming Wailers cult': 'middle-class whites or blacks who want into the capitalist system, not out of it. Do they really enjoy getting high and grooving on images of slave ships, starvation and riots, or are they just dancing to the music?' He also cited an editorial in a 'West Indian entertainment magazine' called *The Caribbean*, which complained bitterly that the press ignored 'Bob's musical talent' to spread 'hocus-pocus' about 'Rastafarianism', 'Dreadlocks', 'Pocomania', 'Haile Selassie', 'Shanty Town'.

That's where Marley stood in American eyes as of the botched assassination of December 3, 1976, which drove him from Jamaica and generated the miraculous outpouring that turned into *Exodus* and *Kaya*. In the stores just six months after the shooting, *Exodus* quickly became Marley's highest-charting UK album, and *Kaya* surpassed it. But in the US, where *Exodus* garnered Marley his first 'urban' airplay, it fell well short of *Rastaman Vibration*'s high-water mark and met critical skepticism. 'Cold and distant,' declared John Morthland in the *Voice*; in *Rolling Stone*, Greil Marcus claimed Marley's singing had lost 'drama' and 'emotion' (he'd said similar things about *Rastaman Vibration*). Once again, popular and critical response shouldn't be confused. If Marley's toe injury hadn't cost him a US tour, the album would have sold more. But the fact remains that Marley's status in America was less stellar than in Britain. Robert Palmer's depiction of Marley's American audience is an impressionistic caricature, as it had to be. But there's no question that where in the UK punk was intertwined with reggae, most US punks barely knew who Marley was. His white US base comprised hippie holdouts of folkie mien, the kind of longhairs who went wild whenever Neil Young sang 'I felt like getting high', while his black fans were West Indians, collegiate Afrocentrists, or both. As

of 1977, he was neither hip nor cool. Moreover, America did have its own black music, and while punks were as stupid about hating disco as Lynyrd Skynyrd fans, less kneejerk rock and rollers were catching on to another rhythmic visionary with rock dreams: George Clinton, a trickster rather than a prophet, but also not someone who would have refused a life-saving amputation or died intestate because he was immortal. It's also fair to point out that by 1977 reggae had produced Marley alternatives less retro than Toots Hibbert: Burning Spear, Culture's 'Two Sevens Clash', the dub that boomed at every punky reggae party.

The question isn't whether *Exodus* is a great album, or whether the American tastemakers who found it wanting made a mistake. It's what kind of great album *Exodus* is. Bemoaning the seven-minute 'Exodus,' Greil Marcus exclaimed, 'If I didn't have more faith in Marley I'd think he was trying to go disco.' Only, as Vivien Goldman explains in *The Book of Exodus*, Marley was trying to go disco: Carlton Barrett deliberately dropped his skanking offbeat for 'the straight, four-on-the-floor propulsion of disco,' and Marley sounds like 'an android' because his voice is run through a vocoder. Watchdogs suspected Marley of abandoning reggae because he was. But that doesn't mean he was betraying it.

Exodus makes something major of the most elusive, and dubious, pop dream: that by targeting the lowest common denominator you can do more than sell product to the masses – you can touch, inspire, and change them. Powered by Marley's instinct for the simple tune, knack for the rousing generalization, and decision to remove 'drama' and 'emotion' – to trade mannerism for control, I'd say – from a voice that never crooned easily, the Wailers joined the select ranks of two bands admired by very few of his white fans and almost none of his critical cadre: drummer-led Africanists Earth, Wind & Fire, and the Commodores, who legend claims the Wailers swamped as an opening act in 1980. Lester Bangs got the idea in his *Rolling Stone* pan of *Kaya* and jumped off a cliff with it: 'This man wants to be a superstar at all costs and will sell out his music, his people, his religion and his politics to get there.'

It's true Marley wanted to be a superstar, and like any leader he had an ego. But he saw fame primarily as a way to spread reggae and the Rasta struggle, and what's more, that's how it worked. Reggae became the beat of international protest because Marley developed his pop gifts – which he then downplayed on Uprising, the best of the post-Kaya albums. His congruences with EWF and the Commodores only underline how much more he achieved, not just culturally but musically. Funkwise, the Wailers and especially the Barrett brothers buried the builders of 'Brick House' and Maurice White's merry men, and Marley achieved woman-friendly presence without sugaring up like Lionel Richie or Philip Bailey. By the end, the Wailers were a rock band, a pop band, an R&B band, a funk band, and a reggae band all at once, sending out the most politically explicit lyrics ever to spice up a tragically premature greatest-hits record, which for a while was on the required listening list of every college freshman in America. Did he radicalize this young army of consumers? Unless you count ganja consciousness, not usually. But only the Beatles and conceivably Elvis Presley can claim as seismic a worldwide social effect. Even if *Exodus* isn't the greatest album of the 20th century, that's saying a lot for a sufferer from the yard.

Marley took the spotlight, but the men in the shadows were vital to the music's success. Behind him, the Barrett brothers – drummer Carlton and bass guitarist Aston – redefined the art of rhythm-section playing, the successors to Benny Benjamin and James Jamerson of the Motown studio band, Al Jackson Jr and Duck Dunn of the Stax house team, and Joseph 'Zigaboo' Modelliste and George Porter of the Meters. Carly and Family Man were among a select group who achieved worldwide respect for Jamaican music.

While Family Man was a
significant figure behind the
scenes in the musical world of the
Wailers, the work of his brother
Carly had drummers all over
the world straining their ears to
analyse his success in providing
such a powerful momentum while
leaving so much space for the
music to breathe. Full of little
surprises, his drumming was
defined by its subtlety.

Right: Throughout his career, Marley's favoured model of electric guitar was a Gibson Les Paul Special with an aged-cherry finish on a mahogany body, a rosewood fretboard on a mahogany neck, single-coil pickups and an aluminium pick-guard.

Left: Don Taylor (left, with Al Anderson, guitarist with the Wailers) was a Jamaican-born hustler who moved to America, where he worked as the soul singer Chuck Jackson's valet and the manager of Little Anthony and the Imperials before returning home to take over the Wailers' management, shortly after the recording of *Catch A Fire*. Of the three victims of the shooting at 56 Hope Road, he suffered the most serious wounds while attempting to shield Marley from the fusillade.

THOUSANDS TURNED OUT TO GREET HIS ARRIVAL AT KINGSTON'S NORMAN MANLEY AIRPORT, THE FIRST TIME HE'D SET FOOT ON HIS BELOVED ISLAND SINCE THE SHOOTING

7 HOMEWARD BOUND

In March 1978, eight months after a Harley Street doctor's diagnosis of cancer in his big toe had forced the postponement of the US leg of the Exodus tour, Bob Marley returned to Jamaica. He had been living away for 15 months, and thousands turned out to greet his arrival at Kingston's Norman Manley Airport, the first time he'd set foot on his beloved island since the shooting. But they were doing more than merely welcoming home a favourite son and, for by now Marley was the most famous Jamaican ever, a world-conquering superstar. The crowds had turned out to meet the man they hoped would save them.

In the months of down time he had mixed the *Kaya* album in Miami and helped his mother, Cedella, move from her home in Wilmington, Delaware, to a mansion in that city. Now he turned his attention to the terrible situation in his homeland. The gun battles on the Kingston streets had continued to escalate as weapons poured in and any moral responsibility on the part of the government had been all but abandoned. Each party continued to hurl rhetoric at the other and covertly fund their Kingston warlords for fear of becoming vulnerable without them, but both had long since lost control of thugs whose chief aim was now little more than gangsterism. The Twelve Tribes Rastafarian organisation had founded something called the Peace Movement at the beginning of that year, as they sought to remind the two sides that their similarities far outweighed their differences. In other words: One Love. It was a concept with which Marley was familiar and, horrified by the situation he'd been reading about, he wanted to get involved.

Around the same time, two of the singer's friends were sharing a Kingston jail cell – Claudie Massop was a JLP warlord, and Bucky Marshall a mid-level PNP gangster. While talking about their mutual acquaintance they came to two conclusions: first, they had too much in common to be trying to kill each other, and second, the state of

HE HAD DONE SO WITH JUST AN UNBENDING SENSE OF PURPOSE,
OF WHAT COULD BE DONE IF PEOPLE ADDRESSED REAL ISSUES
WITH LOGIC AND COMPASSION RATHER THAN THROUGH
POLITICAL MANIFESTOS

war on the ghetto streets was getting in the way of making money out of crime. A gang truce was the obvious way forward, and in their minds Bob Marley was the only man who could bring it about.

The idea of marking a truce with a concert that would coincide with Marley's homecoming, and guaranteed his safety, was put to the singer in Miami after Massop had discussed it with Twelve Tribes representatives who agreed to mediate. As keen to do anything to promote peace as he was to get back safely to Jamaica, Marley agreed – he signed up to the simple proposal that ordinary people such as themselves should take over from the 'politricks' and get something done instead of merely talking about it. He later met with Massop and his PNP equivalent Tony Welch in London, where they hammered out the terms of the Peace Treaty. The date for the concert, April 22, was announced from there in February, and it was against a background of hope and optimism that

Bob Marley's return to Jamaica took on an almost messianic quality. What occurred on that astonishing night of music served to justify such a notion.

By the time the concert kicked off, it had assumed global proportions. The violence in Jamaica had been under the international spotlight since Marley's shooting in 1976, his continued escalating stardom and the socio-political themes of the huge-selling *Exodus* album made sure it stayed there. The idea that a rock star was going to deliver what the government could not, and call off what amounted to a bloody civil war, caught the imagination of the world's press. This was now much more than just a gig, and what happened next shocked everybody involved.

As Marley performed the song 'One Love', he called on the two political leaders, Michael Manley and Edward Seaga, to join him on stage before seizing their hands and joining them above his head in a symbolic gesture of unity. Flashed all

over the world, it was an image that elevated Bob Marley from a mere singer of songs to the status of an international statesman. As a spectacular triumph of the human spirit, it almost made up for the personal pain that preceded it. After nearly a year and a half in exile, Marley's vision for the Smile Jamaica concert had finally come to pass. No matter how brief the moment – and the two politicians didn't linger any longer than the singer's embrace necessitated – Bob Marley had brought peace to Jamaica.

He had done so with just an unbending sense of purpose, of what could be done if people addressed real issues with logic and compassion rather than through political manifestos. And Bob Marley was the only person in the world who could have brought it off.

THE GUN BATTLES ON THE KINGSTON STREETS HAD CONTINUED
TO ESCALATE AS WEAPONS POURED IN AND ANY MORAL
RESPONSIBILITY ON THE PART OF THE GOVERNMENT HAD BEEN
ALL BUT ABANDONED

Marley at 56 Hope Road with his childhood friend Claudius 'Claudie' Massop, an enforcer of Edward Seaga's Jamaican Labour Party, the day before the Peace Concert. Nine months later Massop and two associates were stopped by the police, ordered out of their taxi, and shot dead.

AROUND THE SAME TIME, TWO OF THE SINGER'S FRIENDS WERE
SHARING A KINGSTON JAIL CELL – CLAUDIE MASSOP WAS A JLP
WARLORD, AND BUCKY MARSHALL A MID-LEVEL PNP GANGSTER

UNDER A PINK MOON

NEIL SPENCER

As Saturday, April 22, 1978 approached, Kingston's mood became delirious. The Peace Concert was not the only subject on people's lips – there was always the deteriorating economy, the empty shop shelves, an incident earlier in the week when three looters had been shot dead by police – but the sense of anticipation was tangible. The TV and press crews had been arriving from foreign parts in numbers, even Mick Jagger was in town for the show where Rolling Stones Records' new signing, Peter Tosh, would play.

Along the streets of downtown Kingston, hits like 'The War Is Over' blared out, celebrating the end of months, indeed years, of gun law, during which the city's warren of ghettoes had been riven by the murderous assaults of rival gangs fighting on behalf of the country's two political parties, the right-wing JLP (Jamaican Labour Party) and the socialist People's National Party (PNP). Both Prime Minister Michael Manley of the PNP and the JLP leader Edward Seaga would attend Saturday's concert at Kingston's National Stadium.

Peace had unexpectedly broken out at the beginning of the year, brokered by two of the island's most fearsome gunlords, Claudie Massop, a JLP supporter, and his PNP counterpart, Bucky Marshall. Massop had persuaded Bob Marley back from exile to head the Peace Concert. A showcase of the island's hottest acts, the event had multiple agendas; to commemorate the 12th anniversary of Hailie Selassie's visit to Jamaica in April 1966, to raise money for ghetto sufferers and 'to set the world an example', as Marley tells me at his Hope Road headquarters the day before the show. 'It's a good heart this thing come out of,' he says. 'A good heart. It couldn't come of politics.'

The house at 56 Hope Road has become the hub of the Peace Movement, its sunlit yard milling with activists, idlers, juice vendors and press. A police car noses into the drive, and a pair of flak-jacketed, rifle-toting cops emerge, only to be firmly ushered away by the diminutive figure of Marley, the Trenchtown rebel turned uptown ruler.

Not that anyone is expecting trouble, simply because, as Marley's manager Don Taylor explains, 'The people behind the concert – Claudie, Bucky and them – are the cause of the trouble in the past. Anyone trying anything would just... disappear.'

By five o'clock on Saturday, when the show begins, the only empty seats in the National Stadium belong to VIPs, still to arrive, who have prime position in front of the stage, ahead of the 160 members of the press. Elsewhere the audience is divided into a 'Peace' section ($10 a ticket), 'Love' ($5) and 'Togetherness' ($2), though there are people perched at every vantage point, some 30,000 in all. The weather, overcast and muggy, is almost stifling inside the stadium, around whose perimeter loom banners urging 'BUILD JAMAICA WITH DISCIPLINE', 'UNITE STRUGGLE PRODUCE', slogans borrowed from Castro's Cuba.

The first half of the show is a revolving door of Jamaica's young hitmakers, all backed by Lloyd Parkes and We The People, a well-drilled ensemble with a blazing four-piece horn section. As a UK reggae fan, it's as if my singles box has sprung to life: Leroy Smart bemoaning a 'Ballistic Affair', the Mighty Diamonds crooning 'I Need a Roof Over My Head', Althea and Donna wiggling through 'Uptown Top Ranking', Culture urging 'Stop the Fussing and Fighting', Dillinger, strutting in outlandish red, gold and green stripes, warning 'Son don't take your guns to town'. Then there is the national pin-up, Dennis Brown, whose immaculate suit and silky vocals are in direct lineage from Marvin Gaye.

At the interval Michael Manley and Edward Seaga arrive, just in time to catch Jacob Miller in full cavort. Miller, a roots hero thanks to hits like 'Tired Fe Lick Weed in A Bush', is a comedic, larger than life character, first rolling his ample belly lasciviously before leaping offstage, seizing a policeman's hat and parading down the stage smoking a spliff to wild applause from the crowd. Then Miller brings on a posse of gunmen – Massop, Marshall and more – who career round the stage arm in arm. A few months back they would have been taking pot shots at each other.

After a stately, enjoyable set from Big Youth, Peter Tosh strides onstage attired in a black kung-fu outfit and beret, every inch the untouchable militant. With a redoubtable band that has Sly and Robbie at its rhythmic pulse, Tosh is in tremendous form as he opens with a throbbing version of his old Wailers song, '400 Years' and pounds through solo hits like 'Stepping Razor' and 'Equal Rights', interspersing them with flurries of fiery rhetoric.

Tosh was never going to waste the chance to display his oratory. He prefaces 'Legalise It' with a lengthy and bitter harangue delivered to the dignitaries before him, denouncing the colonial past and slave traders like Henry Morgan, warning against modern-day pirates 'with their camera round their neck', and denouncing the police for 'brutalising poor people for an ickle draw of herb' to a great boom of applause.

It's incendiary stuff, for which Tosh will pay a few months later with a bone-breaking beating from the police. Ras Michael and the Sons of Negus have militant songs, too, but leave them aside for a set of slow Rasta drumming and chanting that shifts the atmosphere inside the stadium to dreamy and devotional. By now the cloud cover has broken and a full moon is sailing magisterially through the Caribbean sky, tinged oddly with pink. 'Even the Moon is red-eye' (stoned), a young dread remarks.

By the time Marley and the Wailers reach the stage it is well past midnight. Bob, wearing a peculiar red, gold and green burlap top with a map of Africa on its back, seems only semi-present, his face drawn, his brow furrowed, his eyes closed. On the opening 'Lion of Judah' his voice also sounds half-there, as if its power has been scraped away by chalice smoke, though it recovers as the group heads into 'Natural Mystic', whose sentiments reverberate sweetly with the night's charged ambience.

The Wailers, their line-up augmented by a horn section and three percussionists, hit their groove well enough, though no-one seems quite able to shake off the slightly strained vibes that have accumulated around the event. I have seen many Marley shows, but this one troubles me. It's as if the immense expectations piled on the singer's wiry shoulders – for in a few short years he has become the ambassador for reggae, Rasta, Jamaica, and dirt-poor millions the world over - are finally taking their toll. Bob has jettisoned his guitar for the night to work the microphone, but his dancing and wild shamanic leaps into the air seem an almost desperate striving for effect.

Still, he and the Wailers surge through 'Trenchtown Rock', 'Natty Dread', 'Positive Vibration' and 'War' without a hitch. Then, as the band segue into 'Jamming', Bob begins to extemporise a rap, calling Manley and Seaga to come onstage with him: 'To show the people that you love them right, to show the people that you gonna unite, show the people that you're over bright, show the people that everything is all right. The moon is high over my head, and I give my love instead...'

The two politicians clamber onstage and, somewhat self-consciously, let Marley raise their clasped hands above his head in a ritual seal of peace and unity. On the fringes of the stage, minders, ghetto gunmen and musicians mill around as the PNP and JLP leaders beam at Marley (certainly not at each other) while the band bursts into 'One Love'. For all that the scenario has been pre-arranged, it's still an extraordinary moment, though arguably less remarkable than the moment three months earlier when their armed representatives agreed to a truce.

As if to remind everyone where he thinks the power behind the occasion is centred, Marley finishes with 'Jah Live', his defiant tribute to Selassie that proves his set's best number. As the audience leaves the stadium, the moon casts our shadows.

Left: Police units receive their briefing as contractors assemble the seating in the National Stadium on the morning of the Peace Concert.

Opposite: A rally in Kingston for Michael Manley's People's National Party, at a time when peace and love were in short supply.

Peter Tosh, who had sung alongside Marley from the formation of the Wailers in 1961 until his departure in 1974, was another star of the Peace Concert.

Left: Here he is at the sound check, with guitarist Earl 'Chinna' Smith (left) and bass guitarist Robbie Shakespeare (right).

Right: Another shot from the sound check at the National Stadium. For the concert itself, Tosh dressed from head to toe in black, lit a spliff on stage, and eyeballed the politicians in the VIP enclosure as he jeered at the 'shitstem'. Less than six months later he was stopped by police on Halfway Tree Road in Kingston and beaten up.

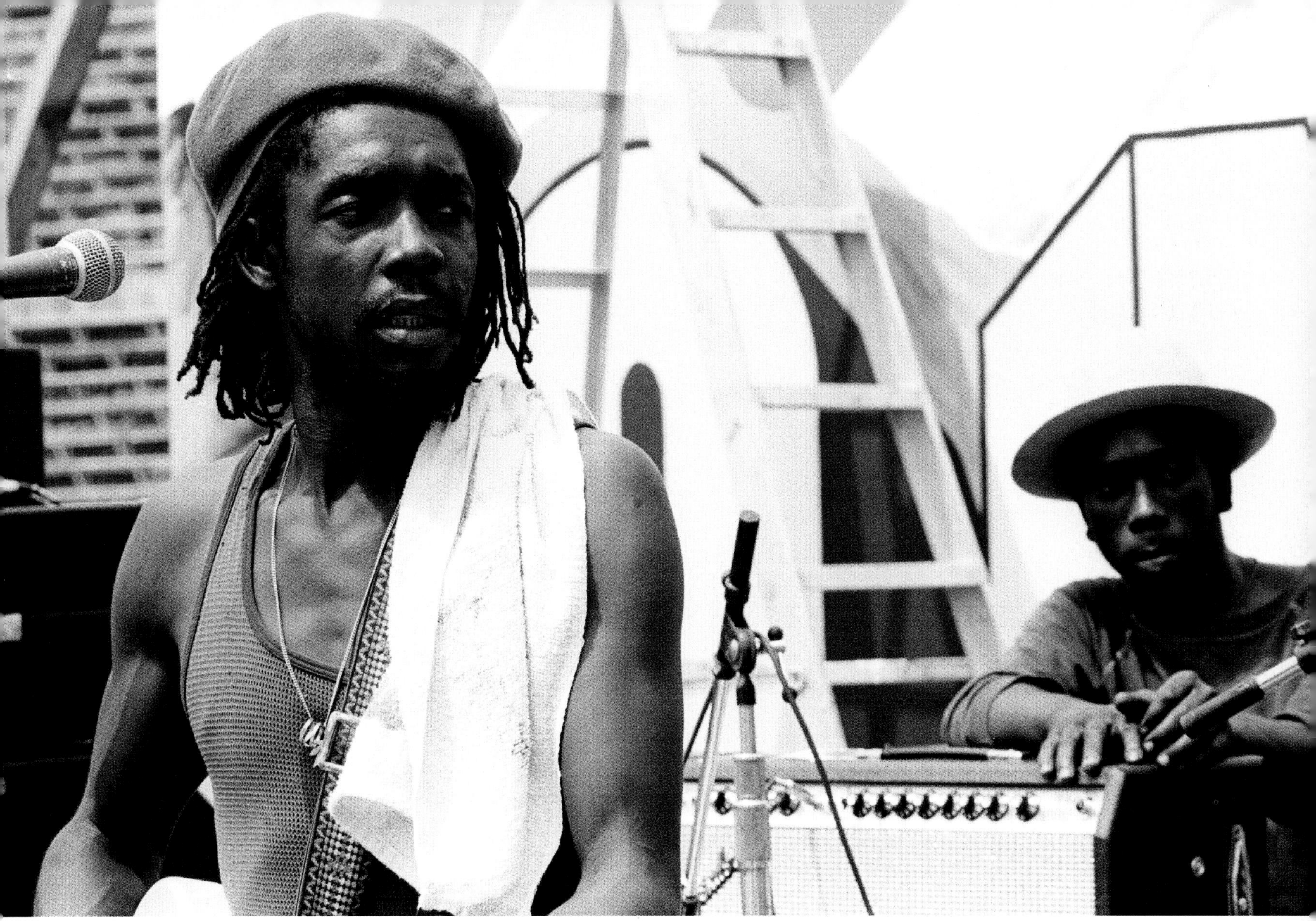

Two kinds of togetherness at the One Love Peace Concert.

Above: Marley and the I-Threes, wearing T-shirts celebrating the release of *Kaya*, the second album compiled from the tracks recorded during the Exodus sessions.

Opposite: Only days away from the general election, Marley overcame the reluctance of the Prime Minister (left) and the Leader of the Opposition (right) to join hands as the concert reached its climax. Over a vamp that segued from 'Jamming' to 'One Love', he rapped: 'His Imperial Majesty Emperor Haile Selassie I, run lightning, leading the people of the slaves to shake hands... To show the people that you love them right, to show the people that you're gonna unite, show the people that you're over bright, show the people that everything is all right... Watch, watch, watch what you're doing, because... I'm not so good at talking, but I hope you understand what I'm trying to say. Could we have, could we have up here on stage the presence of Mr Michael Manley and Mr Edward Seaga. I just want to shake hands and show the people that we're gonna unite... we're gonna unite... we've got to unite... the moon is high over my head, and I give my love instead... the moon is high over my head, and I give my love instead...' Pictures of the moment were flashed around the world.

Marley had been away from
Jamaica for more than a year
when hundreds of fans broke
through security barriers to greet
him as his plane touched down at
Kingston's Norman Manley Airport
on February 26, 1978.
He had returned in order to
discuss plans for a concert which
could provide a symbol of unity.
Three months later the Peace
Concert brought politicians and
gangsters into the same camera
frame, under the world's gaze.
But however noble the intention,
however exhilarating the moment,
it was to prove a fragile success.

Left & right: Marley at the Peace Concert, ending his set with the anthemic 'One Love'.

THE POETRY OF EXILE

LINTON KWESI JOHNSON

I should not have been as pleasantly surprised as I was when Bob Marley's *Exodus* was voted Album of the Century by *Time* magazine. After all, it was the record that propelled Marley, a Jamaican reggae artist, from global stardom to superstar status. Whilst many of his fans would beg to differ with *Time*'s choice, *Exodus* has some of Marley's most memorable tunes and is certainly, lyrically, one of his most uplifting.

A gifted singer/songwriter, Marley often began his songs with a statement of his topic followed by elaboration and conclusion and re-statement in the normal chorus-verse-chorus or verse-chorus-verse structure. Proverbs, aphorisms and sayings of everyday Jamaican speech, together with biblical quotations, provide his metaphors and allusions. Marley's lyrics cannot be read without being heard. His rendition of his songs, the way he uses his voice, provide clues to his meaning. His method of composition is oral and improvisatory.

A purely textual reading of the lyrics from *Exodus* does not illuminate Marley's genius; a contextual reading, however, can be rewarding. *Exodus* was recorded during Marley's exile in London after surviving a politically motivated assassination attempt.[1] The lyrics of the songs

on the album can be read in the context of that traumatic experience. Even though some of the songs were composed before the shooting, it is my contention that, if we exclude the two love songs, the other eight can be read as a sequence that constitute an organic whole, a movement from darkness to light. Two songs connected to the attempt on Marley's life, 'Running Away' and 'Ambush in the Night', appear on the albums *Kaya* and *Survival* respectively, released after

The poet Linton Kwesi Johnson on Railton Road, Brixton, in 1980.

NATURAL MYSTIC

There's a natural mystic blowing through the air
If you listen carefully now you will hear
This could be the first trumpet
Might as well be the last
Many more will have to suffer
Many more will have to die
Don't ask me why

Things are not the way they used to be
I won't tell no lie
One and all got to face reality now
Though I try to find the answers to all the questions they ask
Though I know it's impossible to go living through the past
Don't tell no lie

There's a natural mystic blowing through the air
Can't keep them down
If you listen carefully now you will hear
Such a natural mystic blowing through the air

This could be the first trumpet
Might as well be the last
Many more will have to suffer
Many more will have to die
Don't ask me why

There's a natural mystic blowing through the air
I won't tell no lie
If you listen carefully now you will hear
There's a natural mystic blowing through the air
Such a natural mystic blowing through the air

There's a natural mystic blowing through the air
Such a natural mystic blowing through the air

SO MUCH THINGS TO SAY

Ooh yeah, yeah, yeah
They got so much things to say right now
They got so much things to say
They got so much things to say right now
They got so much things to say

Well I'll never forget, no way, they crucified Jesus Christ
I'll never forget, no way, they sold Marcus Garvey for rice
Ooh and I'll never forget, no, no way
They turned their backs on Paul Bogle
So don't you forget, no youths, who you are
And where you stand in the struggle

They got so much things to say right now (So very, very, so very)
They got so much things to say
They got so much things to say right now (So much things to say)
They got so much things to say

I and I no come to fight flesh and blood
But spiritual wickedness in high and low places
So while they fight you down stand firm

And give Jah thanks and praises
'Cause I and I don't expect to be justified
By the laws of man, by the laws of man
Oh the jury found me guilty but truth, truth
Shall prove my innocence
Oh when the rain falls it don't fall on one man's house
Just remember that
When the rain falls it don't fall on one man's house
They're singing

So very much things to say right now
They got so much things to say
They're singing
So much things to say right now
They got so much things to say

But I and I, I and I no come to fight flesh and blood
But spiritual wickedness in high and low places
So while, so while, so while they fight you down stand firm
And give Jah thanks and praises

I and I don't expect to be justified
By the laws of men, by the laws of men
It takes true God to prove my innocence
I know the wicked think they found me guilty

They got so much to say right now
Well, well, well, well, well, well, well, well
So much things to say
So much things right now
So much things to say

Rumours about
They got rumours without humour
They don't know what they're doing
Yeah

GUILTINESS

Guiltiness (Talking 'bout guiltiness)
Rest on their conscience (Oh yes. Oh yes)
And they live a life of false pretence every day
Each and every day

These are the big fish (These are the big fish)
Who always try to eat down the small fish (Just the small fish)
I tell you again. They would do anything
To materialise their every wish
Oh yeah. But wait!
Woe to the downpressers. They'll eat the bread of sorrow
Woe to the downpressers. They'll eat the bread of sad tomorrow
Woe to the downpressers. They'll eat the bread of sorrow
Oh yeah. Oh yeah

Guiltiness (Talking 'bout guiltiness)
Rest on their conscience (Oh yeah. Oh yes)

These are the big fish (These are the big fish)
Who always try to eat down the small fish
A just the small fish (I'll tell you what)

They would do anything (Anything)
To materialise their every wish
Oh yeah

But woe
Woe to the downpressers. They'll eat the bread of sorrow
Woe to the downpressers. They'll eat the bread of sad tomorrow
Woe to the downpressers. They'll eat the bread of sad tomorrow
Oh yeah. Oh yeah

Guiltiness. Oh yeah
Oh they'll eat the bread of sorrow (Every day)
Every day they'll eat the bread of sad tomorrow (Every day)

Exodus. However, the choice of 'Natural Mystic', 'Guiltiness', 'Three Little Birds' and 'One Love' only become significant in the light of the assassination attempt. It is in Marley's Rastafarian faith, and his implacable belief in a 'natural mystic', that we locate the thematic thread, as we are taken through songs about faith, betrayal, persecution, defiance, resistance, recuperation, love and hope.

The album opens with the brooding melancholy of 'Natural Mystic', a prelude that foregrounds the songs that follow. It is a meditation on life's contradictions and the intractability of their resolution. Here the mood is one of despondency in the face of a cycle of suffering: 'Many more will have to suffer/Many more will have to die.' The fatalism of these lines is tempered by faith. The persona of the song declares that his statement of gloom cannot be explained – 'Don't ask me why' – but immediately gives an explanation: 'There's a natural mystic blowing through the air.'

This simple statement of belief when confronted with the perplexities of life's trials and tribulations is followed by 'So Much Things to Say', the first song on the album that speaks directly to the assassination attempt and speculation about its cause. It is a powerful riposte to the rumour-mongers who had cast aspersions on Marley's character, one which finds him in a lyrically combative and self-assertive mood. His theme here is betrayal and persecution. The names of Jamaican national heroes Marcus Garvey and Paul Bogle as well as Jesus Christ – all iconic figures of betrayal and persecution – are invoked. He

THE HEATHEN

De heathen back dey 'pon de wall!
De heathen back, yeah, 'pon de wall!
De heathen back dey 'pon de wall!
De heathen back, yeah, 'pon de wall!

Rise up fallen fighters
Rise and take your stance again
'Tis he who fight and run away
Live to fight another day.

With de heathen back dey 'pon de wall!
De heathen back, yeah, 'pon de wall!
De heathen back dey 'pon de wall!
De heathen back, yeah, 'pon de wall!

As a man sow, shall he reap
And I know that talk is cheap
But the hotter the battle
A the sweeter Jah victory

With de heathen back dey 'pon de wall!
De heathen back, yeah, 'pon de wall!
De heathen back dey 'pon de wall!
De heathen back, yeah, 'pon de wall!

De heathen back dey 'pon de wall!
De heathen back, yeah, 'pon de wall!
De heathen back dey 'pon de wall!
De heathen back, yeah, 'pon de wall!

Rise up, fallen fighters:
Rise and take your stance again.
'Tis he who fight and run away
Live to fight another day.

De heathen back dey 'pon de wall!
De heathen back, yeah, 'pon de wall!
De heathen back dey 'pon de wall!
De heathen back, yeah, 'pon de wall!
De heathen back dey 'pon de wall!
De heathen back, yeah, 'pon de wall!
De heathen back dey 'pon de wall!
De heathen back, yeah, 'pon de wall!
De heathen back dey 'pon de wall!
De heathen back, yeah, 'pon de wall!

EXODUS

Exodus
Movement of Jah people. Oh yeah

Open your eyes and let me tell you this
Men and people will fight you down
Tell me why!
When you see Jah light
Let me tell you if you're not wrong
Then why?
Everything is alright
So we gonna walk. Alright
Through the roads of creation

We're the generation
Tell me why!
Trod through great tribulation

Exodus. Movement of Jah people
Exodus. Movement of Jah people

Open your eyes
And look within
Are you satisfied
With the life you're living?
We know where we're going
We know where we're from
We're leaving Babylon
We're going to our Father's land

Exodus. Movement of Jah people

Movement of Jah people
Send us another brother Moses
Movement of Jah people
Gonna cross the Red Sea
Movement of Jah people
Send us another brother Moses
Movement of Jah people
Gonna cross the Red Sea
Movement of Jah people

Exodus. Movement of Jah people
Exodus. Exodus. Exodus. Exodus
Exodus. Exodus. Exodus. Exodus

Move! Move! Move!
Move! Move! Move!

Open your eyes and look within
Are you satisfied
With the life you're living?
We know where we're going
We know where we're from
We're leaving Babylon
We're going to our Father's land

Exodus. Movement of Jah people
Exodus. Movement of Jah people

Movement of Jah people
Movement of Jah people
Movement of Jah people
Movement of Jah people

Move! Move! Move!
Move! Move! Move!
Move!

Jah come to break downpression
Rule equality
Wipe away transgression
Set the captives free

Exodus. Movement of Jah people
Exodus. Movement of Jah people
Movement of Jah people
Movement of Jah people

JAMMING

Well alright. We're jammin'
I wanna jam it with you
We're jammin', jammin'
And I hope you like jammin' too

Ain't no rules, ain't no vow
We can do it anyhow
I and I will see you through
'Cause every day we pay the price
We're the living sacrifice
Jammin' till the jam is through

We're jammin'
To think that jammin' was a thing of the past
We're jammin'
And I hope this jam is gonna last

No bullet can stop us now
We neither beg nor we won't bow
Neither can be bought nor sold
We all defend the right
Jah Jah children must unite
For life is worth much more than gold

We're jammin (Jammin', jammin', jammin')
And we're jammin' in the name of the Lord
We're jammin' (Jammin', jammin' jammin')
We're jammin' right straight from Yard

Holy Mount Zion. Holy Mount Zion
Jah seateth in Mount Zion and rules
  all creation

Yeah, we're, we're jammin'
Scatting. We're jammin'
I wanna jam it with you
We're jammin' (Jammin, jammin, jammin')
And Jamdown hope you're jammin' too

Jah knows how much I've tried
The truth I cannot hide
To keep you satisfied
True love that now exists
Is the love I can't resist
So jam by my side

We're jammin' (Jammin', jammin', jammin')
I wanna jam it with you
We're jammin', we're jammin', we're jammin',
we're jammin'
We're jammin', we're jammin', we're jammin,
we're jammin'
Hope you like jammin' too

implores the youth to remember 'who you are and where you stand in the struggle', and declares that his fight is against 'spiritual wickedness in high and low places'. Towards the end of the song he employs mockery as a tool of derision against his detractors.

'Guiltiness', written before the assassination attempt, prefigures the event and reads like a comment on the crime. A bitter song of vengeance, it fits neatly in the sequence of songs. 'Guiltiness' is a visceral indictment of 'the big fish' who 'would do anything to materialise their every wish'. Marley takes on a prophetic voice as he cries 'woe to the downpresser' whose lot will be 'the bread of sorrow'.

'The Heathen' is a good example of the economy of Marley's lyricism and his deft use of biblical metaphor and allusion for rhetorical effect. With its portentous bass line, 'The Heathen' is a powerful yet simple statement of defiance and reaffirmation. Inspired by the attempt on Marley's life, it is a call to arms: 'Rise up fallen fighters/Rise and take your stance again/Tis he who fights and run away/Live to fight another day.' Here the personal need for a boost in morale becomes a collective stance of defiance addressed to 'fallen fighters'. But it is the

WAITING IN VAIN

I don't wanna wait in vain for your love
I don't wanna wait in vain for your love

From the very first time I placed my eyes
*   on you girl*
My heart says follow through
But I know now that I'm way down on your line
But the waiting feel is fine
So don't treat me like a puppet on a string
'Cause I know how to do my thing
Don't talk to me as if you think I'm dumb
I wanna know when you're gonna come

See I don't wanna wait in vain for your love
I don't wanna wait in vain for your love
I don't wanna wait in vain for your love
'Cause it's summer is here
I'm still waiting there
Winter is here
And I'm still waiting there

Like I said
It's been three years since I'm knocking
*   on your door*
And I still can knock some more
Ooh girl, ooh girl, is it feasible
I wanna know now
For I to knock some more?
You see
In life I know there is lots of grief
But your love is my relief
Tears in my eyes burn
Tears in my eyes burn
While I'm waiting
While I'm waiting for my turn

See I don't wanna wait in vain for your love
I don't wanna wait in vain for your love
I don't wanna wait in vain for your love
I don't wanna wait in vain for your love
I don't wanna wait in vain for your love
Oh I don't wanna, I don't wanna, I don't wanna
I don't wanna, I don't wanna wait in vain
No I don't wanna, I don't wanna, I don't wanna
I don't wanna, I don't wanna wait in vain

I don't wanna, I don't wanna, I don't wanna
I don't wanna, I don't wanna wait in vain
I don't wanna, I don't wanna, I don't wanna
I don't wanna, I don't wanna wait in vain

It's your love that I'm waiting on
It's my love that you're running from
It's your love that I'm waiting on
It's my love that you're running from

TURN YOUR LIGHTS DOWN LOW

Turn your lights down low
And pull your window curtains
Oh, let Jah moon come shining in
Into our life again,

Sayin': ooh, it's been a long, long
(long, long, long, long) time
I kept this message for you, girl,
But it seems I was never on time
Still I wanna get through to you, girlie
On time - on time.

I want to give you some love (good, good lovin');
I want to give you some good, good lovin'
(good, good lovin').
Oh, I - oh, I - oh, I,
Say, I want to give you some good, good lovin'
(good, good lovin'):

Turn your lights down low
Never try to resist, oh no!
Oh, let my love come tumbling in
Into our life again,
Sayin': ooh, I love ya!
And I want you to know right now
I love ya!
And I want you to know right now
'Cause I - that I -

I want to give you some love, oh - ooh!
I want to give you some good, good lovin'
Oh, I - I want to give you some love
Sayin': I want to give you some good, good lovin'

Turn your lights down low, wo - oh!
Never - never try to resist, oh no!
Ooh, let my love - ooh, let my love
*   come tumbling in -*
Into our life again.
Oh, I want to give you some good, good lovin'
(good, good lovin').

THREE LITTLE BIRDS

Don't worry about a thing
'Cause every little thing gonna be alright
Singing
Don't worry about a thing
'Cause every little thing gonna be alright

Rise up this morning
Smiled with the rising sun
Three little birds pitch by my doorstep
Singing sweet songs of melodies pure and true
Saying
This is my message to you

Singing
Don't worry about a thing
'Cause every little thing gonna be alright
Singing
Don't worry about a thing
'Cause every little thing gonna be alright

Rise up this morning
Smiled with the rising sun
Three little birds pitch by my doorstep
Singing sweet songs of melodies pure and true
Saying
This is my message to you

Singing
Don't worry about a thing
'Cause every little thing gonna be alright

ONE LOVE / PEOPLE GET READY

One love. One heart
Let's get together and feel alright
Hear the children crying (One love)
Hear the children crying (One heart)
Saying
Give thanks and praise to the Lord and I
*   will feel alright*
Saying
Let's get together and feel alright

Let them all pass all their dirty remarks (One love)
There is one question I'd really love to ask
*   (One heart)*
Is there a place for the hopeless sinner
Who has hurt all mankind just to save his own?
Believe me

One love
What about the one heart?
One heart
What about...
Let's get together and feel alright
As it was in the beginning (One love)
So shall it be in the end (One heart)
Alright
Give thanks and praise to the Lord and I
*   will feel alright*
Let's get together and feel alright

One more thing
Let's get together to fight this holy Armageddon
(One love)
So when the Man comes there will be no, no doom
(One song)
Have pity on those whose chances grows thinner
There ain't no hiding place from the Father of
Creation

Saying
One love
What about the one heart?
One heart
What about the...
Let's get together and feel alright
I'm pleading to mankind
One love. Oh, Lord
One heart
Give thanks and praise to the Lord and I
*   will feel alright*
Let's get together and feel alright
Give thanks and praise to the Lord and I
*   will feel alright*
Let's get together and feel alright
Let them get together and feel alright

repetition of the one-line chorus – 'de heathen back dey 'pon de wall' – that gives the song its hypnotic sense of dread.

'Exodus' and 'Jamming', the other two songs in the sequence that relate to the assassination attempt, are both celebratory. 'Exodus' signals a shift in mood from the sombre musing of the earlier songs to a more upbeat mood. Here Marley delights in the rightness of his cause, the right-eousness of his vision of redemption, underpinned by the Garveyite project of repatriation. He celebrates the Rastafarian movement to which he belongs, a movement of like-minded souls who have 'trod through great tribulation' and seen 'Jah light'. 'Exodus' is ultimately a song of faith and yet it speaks to the sense of alienation that comes with the postmodern experience of mass migration and global diasporas.

'Jamming' communicates the sheer exhilaration Marley must have felt having escaped death and the demons that came in the wake of his traumatic experience as he embarked on a new stage of his career. Notwithstanding the obvious sexual connotation, 'Jamming' is employed here as a metaphor of togetherness and unity ('Jah Jah children must unite'). It is a song that celebrates

life and is a statement of reaffirmation. With confidence Marley declares 'No bullets can stop us now/We won't beg nor we won't bow/Neither can be bought or sold.' That confidence is an expression of faith born of experience.

'Waiting in Vain' and 'Turn Your Lights Down Low' allow for a romantic interlude in the sequence of songs. These two songs of seduction can also be read as recuperative, avoiding a breach in the sequence. 'Waiting in Vain' (an all-time favourite of mine), with its invigorating bass line, is a plea for love reminiscent of the Impressions' 'Minstrel and Queen', rock-steady versioned as 'Queen Majesty' by the Techniques. However, the supplicant in Marley's song is no mere humble minstrel. Marley's rhetoric of seduction is finely balanced between coyness and confidence, between uncertainty and resolve. The chorus line – 'I don't wanna wait in vain for your love' – is both plea and veiled threat. The humility of 'I know that I'm way down on your line' is contrasted by 'I know how to do my thing' and 'It's my love that you're running from.'[2] 'Turn Your Lights Down Low' pales in comparison with 'Waiting in Vain', both lyrically and musically. This bedroom ballad of rekindled love lacks conviction. The repeated line of desire 'I want to give you some good, good loving' would perhaps be more convincing had it been one of intent: 'I'm gonna give you some good, good loving.'

'Three Little Birds' and 'One Love' reconnect and complete the song sequence. 'Three Little Birds' is a song of hope; a catchy chorus that is at once infectious. Its simple message of reassurance – 'Don't worry about a thing/'Cause every little thing gonna be alright' – immediately touches a universal chord. The imagery of three little birds is endearing. 'One Love', an old Wailers' song inspired by Curtis Mayfield, again finds Marley in an exuberant mood. This song of praise, rejoicing and giving thanks, a plea for brotherly and sisterly love and a re-statement of faith is an apt ending. By the time we get to 'One Love' we have been taken through a range of moods and emotions that have journeyed us from despair to hope, in a movement from darkness to light. Marley's 'lyrical genius'[3] lies in his ability to

translate the personal into the political, the private into the public, the particular into the universal with a seeming simplicity that guarantees accessibility. The lyrics of the songs from *Exodus* are ample evidence of this.

Notes
1. Goldman, Vivien. *The Book of Exodus*.
London: Aurum Press, 2006.
2. For an alternative reading of 'Waiting in Vain' see 'Slackness Personified' in Cooper, Carolyn, *Sound Clash: Jamaican Dancehall Culture at Large*.
New York: Palgrave Macmillan, 2004.
3. Dawes, Kwame. *Bob Marley: Lyrical Genius*.
London: Sanctuary, 2002.

Exodus was released in the UK on June 3, 1977. The following month, with most of the Wailers back in Jamaica, Marley and the producer Lee 'Scratch' Perry assembled a scratch band of musicians from Third World and Aswad and recorded 'Punky Reggae Party' in London. Perry subsequently took the multitrack tape back to Kingston, overdubbing horns and voices before meeting Marley in Miami to make a final mix. Perry then took the tapes back to Jamaica, where he created another mix which he released on his own Black Ark label.

The *Kaya* album, drawn from the sessions that had produced *Exodus*, appeared early in 1978, delivering two more hit singles, 'Satisfy My Soul' and 'Is This Love'. By that time, believing that his cancer had been cured, Marley visited New York, where he received the United Nations' Medal of Peace. He and the Wailers resumed touring, visiting Europe and the United States. He also made his first trip to Africa, including stops in Kenya and Ethiopia.

When they recorded again, it was in Jamaica once more. A new studio was created in the house at 56 Hope Road, and a new album, *Survival*, was released early in 1979, including such militant anthems as 'Zimbabwe' and 'Africa Unite', which took on an added significance when, invited by Robert Mugabe, they performed at Zimbabwe's Independence celebrations in April 1980. A month later came the release of their final studio album, *Uprising*, which included the hit 'Could You Be Loved' and the classic 'Redemption Song'. The band toured Europe and America, but it was after two concerts at Madison Square Garden in New York that Marley collapsed while jogging in Central Park. The next eight months were occupied by a fight for survival, much of it conducted in a Bavarian clinic. It was on his way home from Germany to Jamaica that he died in Miami on May 11, 1981, aged 36. Ten days later a state funeral brought his native land to a standstill.

Opposite: Marley at the mixing desk of the studio installed in the house at Hope Road following his return to Jamaica in 1978, his period of exile at an end.

Right: Denise Mills and Bob Marley at the back of 56 Hope Road. When they first met, Denise was Chris Blackwell's executive assistant at Island Records. She became Bob's friend and confidante, the person whom he trusted implicitly to make whatever arrangements he and the band required during their visits to the UK and Europe. It was she who, in July 1977, accompanied him to a Harley Street consultant's office, where he was told that he was suffering from cancer. After his death she went to live in Jamaica but in 1994, following a diagnosis of emphysema, she returned to the UK, where she died that year.

Neville Garrick, Tuff Gong's art director, carries his boom-box through the shallows on the beach at Goldeneye, near the village of Oracabessa on Jamaica's north coast.

CONTRIBUTORS

ADRIAN BOOT After leaving university in 1970, Adrian Boot taught physics in Jamaica before returning to London to become one of Britain's best known music photographers, working for the *NME*, the *Melody Maker*, *The Face* and many other publications, his subjects ranging from the Grateful Dead to Nelson Mandela. Over the last 10 years he has become involved in the fusion of photography with digital technology, working with Palm Pictures on various DVD, internet, film and CDR projects. His books include *Babylon on a Thin Wire* (with Michael Thomas) and *Bob Marley – Songs of Freedom* (with Chris Salewicz).

LLOYD BRADLEY Lloyd Bradley is author of *Bass Culture: When Reggae Was King,* a former sound system owner and operator, was associate producer of BBC2's *Reggae: The Story Of Jamaican Music* and is a regular contributor to *Mojo* magazine. He was trained as a chef at the Caprice, sang on one of Bootsy Collins's albums and has only ever lived on two pages of the A-Z, always within walking distance of Highbury.

ROBERT CHRISTGAU A longtime *Village Voice* editor and critic, Robert Christgau is now a contributing editor at *Rolling Stone* and a critic at National Public Radio's *All Things Considered*. His Consumer Guide appears at MSN Music and most of his work can be read at robertchristgau.com.

VIVIEN GOLDMAN Vivien Goldman is a writer, broadcaster, educator and musician specializing in punk and Afro-Caribbean music and culture. In *The Book Of Exodus* she focuses on Bob Marley between 1975-8: the assassination attempt, recording of *Exodus*, and the Peace Concert.

Goldman also wrote the first biography of Marley, *Soul Rebel, Natural Mystic*. Shortly after leaving Warwick University, Goldman was briefly Marley's PR at Island Records, and then covered the Wailers frequently as a writer. Her journalism appears in the *New York Times*, the *New Statesman*, *Rolling Stone*, the *Observer*, etc. She is the Adjunct Professor of Punk and Reggae at New York University.

LINTON KWESI JOHNSON Linton Kwesi Johnson is a Jamaican-born poet, reggae artist and writer. He runs his own record label, LKJ Records, and LKJ Music Publishers. His most recent recordings are *More Time* and *LKJ Live in Paris with the Dennis Bovell Dub Band*. His most recent books are *Selected Poems* and *Mi Revalueshanary Fren*.

DENNIS MORRIS Brought up in the East End of London, Dennis Morris caught the camera bug as a child and was 11 years old when his photograph of a PLO demonstration appeared on the front page of the *Daily Mirror*. Bunking off school to sneak into the Wailers' soundcheck at the Speakeasy Club in 1973, he was befriended by Bob Marley. Subsequently he became the Sex Pistols' official photographer and the art director for Public Image Ltd. As a musician, he performed with the bands Basement 5, Urban Shakedown and Boss. He is currently involved with TV projects.

KATE SIMON Kate Simon first met Bob Marley at a party in London after the Wailers' shows at the Lyceum in 1975. The following year her first visit to Jamaica produced the cover shot of *Kaya*, and in 1977 she accompanied Marley and the band on the Exodus tour. Her images of Marley were collected in the book *Rebel Music: Bob Marley & Roots Reggae*. Among her many other subjects have been Paul Simon, Patti Smith, Eric Clapton, Debbie Harry, Burning Spear, Madonna and William Burroughs. She is married to the singer David Johansson and lives in New York.

NEIL SPENCER Neil Spencer interviewed Bob Marley several times while working for the *New Musical Express*, first as a feature writer and later, from 1978-85, as the paper's editor. Subsequently he was a founding editor of *Straight No Chaser* and *Arena* magazines, before becoming a music critic for the *Observer*. He also contributes to *Uncut* and *Rock & Folk*. He is the scriptwriter of *Bollywood Queen*, 'Britain's first masala musical' and a Sundance Festival entry.

STYLOROUGE Founded in 1981 by Rob O'Connor, the Stylorouge design studio has worked on many Bob Marley projects since the singer's death, including CD and DVD packaging, film posters, and an exhibition of photographs which has toured galleries in Europe, Africa, the United States and Australasia.

RICHARD WILLIAMS In 1972 Richard Williams wrote about the Wailers after attending the *Catch A Fire* sessions in Jamaica on behalf of the *Melody Maker*. He has been on the staff of *Time Out*, *The Times* (for which he covered Marley's funeral) and the *Independent on Sunday*, and has contributed to *Granta*, *Mojo*, the *TLS* and many other publications. Since 1995 he has been the chief sports writer of the *Guardian*. His writings on music were collected in *Long Distance Call*.

CREDITS & ACKNOWLEDGEMENTS

1 **NATURAL MYSTIC** 3.28

2 **SO MUCH THINGS TO SAY** 3.08

3 **GUILTINESS** 3.19

4 **THE HEATHEN** 2.32

5 **EXODUS** 7.40

6 **JAMMING** 3.31

7 **WAITING IN VAIN** 4.16

8 **TURN YOUR LIGHTS DOWN LOW** 3.39

9 **THREE LITTLE BIRDS** 3.00

10 **ONE LOVE / PEOPLE GET READY** 2.52

EXTRA TRACKS

11 **JAMMING** 5.52

12 **PUNKY REGGAE PARTY** 6.50

Long versions

Album credits

All tracks written by Bob Marley and published by Fifty-Six Hope Road Music Ltd / Odnil Music Ltd / Blue Mountain Music Ltd Except 'One Love / People Get Ready', written by Bob Marley / Curtis Mayfield and published by Fifty-Six Hope Road Music Ltd / Odnil Music Ltd / Blue Mountain Music Ltd / Warner-Tamerlane Music Pub Corp / Warner/Chappell North America; and 'Punky Reggae Party', written by Bob Marley / Lee Perry and published by Fifty-Six Hope Road Music / Odnil Music Ltd / Blue Mountain Music Ltd / New Town Sound Ltd

Bob Marley: lead vocal, rhythm guitar, acoustic guitar, percussion
Aston 'Family Man' Barrett: bass guitar, guitar, percussion
Carlton Barrett: drums, percussion
Tyrone Downie: keyboards, percussion, backing vocals
Alvin 'Seeco' Patterson: percussion
Julian 'Junior' Marvin: lead guitar
David Madden: trumpet
Glen DaCosta: saxophone
Vin Gordon: trombone
Rita Marley, Marcia Griffiths
& Judy Mowatt (The I Threes): backing vocals

Recorded at the Fallout Shelter, London, January-February 1977
Mixed at Basing Street Studios, London, March-April 1977
Engineer: Karl Pitterson.
Assistants: Guy Bidmead and Terry Barham.
Mixed by Aston Barrett, Chris Blackwell and Karl Pitterson.
Produced by Bob Marley & the Wailers

Tracks 1-10 originally released in the UK as Island ILPS 9498 on June 3, 1977

℗ 1977 Island Records /Universal Music

Book credits

This book was produced by The Island Trading Co Ltd: Suzette Newman, Adrian Boot

Editorial: Chris Blackwell, Lloyd Bradley, Robert Christgau, Vivien Goldman; author of *The Book of Exodus* (Aurum Press), Linton Kwesi Johnson, Neil Spencer, Richard Williams (editor)

Copy-editor: Jackie Strachan, JMS Books

Design by Stylorouge. Cover design based on original *Exodus* sleeve design by Neville Garrick. Design director: David Rowley

Special thanks to Michael Dover at Orion, Chris Blackwell, Bob Marley Music, Jon Turner, Olivier Robert Murphy at Island / Universal, Cassie Williams, Mark Painter, Blue Mountain Music, Rob O'Connor and Mikkel Lundsager Hansen at Stylorouge

And with thanks for their contributions to Rob Partridge, John Knowles, Julian Alexander, Richard Horsey – urbanimage picture research, Kate Simon and Trevor Wyatt

Lyrics reproduced by kind permission of Blue Mountain Music Ltd. www.bluemountainmusic.tv

Colour reproduction by DL Interactive UK
Printed and bound in Italy by Rotolito Lombarda SpA
Typeset in Deadwood and Reykjavik from Psy/ops

www.bobmarley.com

First published in Great Britain in 2007
by Weidenfeld & Nicolson
10 9 8 7 6 5 4 3 2 1

Text copyright © Fifty-Six Hope Road Music Ltd. / Blue Mountain Music 2006
Image copyrights as per photographic credits list
Design & layout © Weidenfeld & Nicolson 2007

Illustration by Ian Wright for the *Songs of Freedom* box set.

Weidenfeld & Nicolson
The Orion Publishing Group Ltd
Orion House
5 Upper St Martin's Lane
London, WC2H 9EA

The Orion Publishing Group's policy is to use papers that are natural, renewable and recyclable products and made from a wood grown in sustainable forests. The logging and manufacturing processes are expected to conform to the environmental regulations of the country of origin

CD cataloged as
separate item

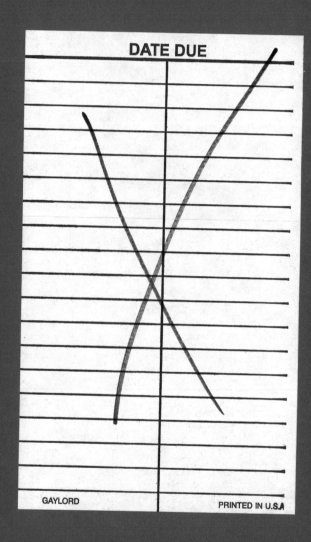